Using Accounting and Financial Information

Using Accounting and Financial Information

Analyzing, Forecasting, and Decision Making

Second Edition

Mark S. Bettner

Using Accounting and Financial Information, Second Edition: Analyzing, Forecasting, and Decision Making

First published in 2018 by
Business Expert Press, LLC
222 East 46th Street, New York, NY 10017
www.businessexpertpress.com

ISBN-13: 978-1-94709-868-8 (paperback)
ISBN-13: 978-1-94709-869-5 (e-book)

Business Expert Press Financial Accounting and Auditing Collection

Collection ISSN: 2151-2795 (print)
Collection ISSN: 2151-2817 (electronic)

Cover and interior design by S4Carlisle Publishing Services
Private Ltd., Chennai, India

First edition: 2015

10 9 8 7 6 5 4 3 2 1

Printed in the United States of America.

Dedication

This book is dedicated to my friends Spot and Buckwheat.

Abstract

Accounting is often referred to as the language of business; unfortunately, many business professionals lack the fluency in this unique language required to perform basic financial analysis, prepare budgetary forecasts, or compare competing capital investment alternatives. And while there is no shortage of financial-related textbooks or reference manuals, most assume that readers have educational backgrounds—and/or have had years of professional experience—in accounting, financial analysis, or corporate finance.

This book targets professionals with limited exposure to—or formal training in—accounting or related finance disciplines. These individuals often include—but certainly are not limited to—engineers, information technology specialists, retail managers, entrepreneurs, marketing directors, construction contractors, attorneys, and even bankers who are making career transitions from consumer lending positions to become commercial loan officers.

The primary purpose of this book is to help managers and business owners from diverse professional and educational backgrounds to (1) converse more effectively with their accounting and finance colleagues; (2) understand the structure and the elements of general purpose financial statements; (3) identify both the usefulness and the limitations of accounting information; (4) prepare basic financial forecasts; and (5) make sense of commonly used decision-making models.

Keywords

accounting, accruals, assets, balance sheet, breakeven, budgeting, capital budgeting, cash flow, cost–volume–profit analysis, decision making, deferrals, discounted present value, equity, expenses, financial analysis, financial forecasting, financial management, financial statements, income statement, internal rate of return, liabilities, liquidity, net present value, payback period, pro forma financial statements, profitability, revenue, solvency, statement of cash flows, time-value of money

Contents

Acknowledgments

I acknowledge the Securities and Exchange Commission (SEC), the Public Company Accounting Oversight Board (PCAOB), the American Institute of Certified Public Accountants (AICPA), and each of the Big Four accounting firms for permission to reference their names and to site their professional standards.

I am grateful for the input that I received from my undergraduate students at Bucknell University who used an earlier edition of this book in their classes. I particularly wish to acknowledge Christi Shingara for the insightful feedback that she provided throughout the revision process. Finally, I thank everyone at Business Expert Press and S4Carlisle Publishing Services—including Scott Isenberg, Michael Coyne, and Rene Caroline Balan—for their ongoing support, encouragement, and professionalism.

CHAPTER 1

Users of Accounting and Financial Information

Accounting is often referred to as *the language of business*; unfortunately, many business professionals lack fluency in this unique language, making it difficult for them to perform basic financial analysis, prepare budgetary forecasts, or compare competing capital investment alternatives. Although there is no shortage of well-written accounting textbooks, budgeting handbooks, or finance publications, most require that readers have educational backgrounds and/or professional experience in accounting and financial management.

This book targets individuals in management positions with limited exposure to—or formal training in—the disciplines of accounting and finance. These professionals include engineers, information technology specialists, entrepreneurs, marketing managers, construction contractors, attorneys, and even bankers who have transitioned from consumer-lending positions to become commercial loan officers.

Throughout this book, accounting and financial reporting subjects are addressed from a *user's* perspective. Thus, topics such as transaction analysis, journal entries, and numerous other recordkeeping procedures associated with financial statement preparation are avoided. Its purpose is to help managers from diverse professional and educational backgrounds to: (1) converse more effectively with their accounting and finance colleagues, (2) appreciate the usefulness and limitations of general purpose financial statements, (3) use accounting information in decision-making processes, (4) develop short- and long-term financial forecasts, and (5) make sense of commonly used decision-making models.

The Role of Accounting in Organizations and Society

A primary objective of accounting is to communicate relevant and reliable information to decision makers that is useful in managing economic resources. This book addresses the role of accounting as it relates to for-profit corporations; however, accounting plays an important role in all types of enterprises—including partnerships, family-owned businesses, nonprofit organizations, and governmental entities.

Users of accounting information include investors, creditors, managers, regulatory agencies, tax authorities, and anyone else interested in financial issues related to a company's efficiency, performance, competitive advantage, and sustainability. When accounting information is prepared for users *external* to an organization (such as investors, creditors, and regulators), it is often referred to as *financial accounting* or *financial reporting.* When it is prepared for users *inside* of an organization (including managers, chief financial officers, board members, and controllers), it is generally referred to as *managerial accounting.* Chapters 2 through 4 devote coverage to external reporting topics, whereas Chapters 5 through 8 focus on internal accounting issues.[1]

Financial Management Systems

It is useful to frame a preliminary discussion of accounting in the context of *financial management systems.*[2] Figure 1.1 illustrates the function of a financial management system as it relates to external and internal decision makers.

Organizations engage in a multitude of economic events and transactions every day. Most of these activities result in the creation of what is referred to in Figure 1.1 as *unprocessed "raw" financial data.* This information often takes the form of source documents such as sales receipts, utility bills, property tax notices, employee timecards, bank statements,

[1]Accounting information communicated to tax authorities requires specialized expertise in the area of *tax accounting.* Tax accounting issues are beyond the scope of this book.

[2]The terms *financial management systems* and *accounting information systems* are frequently used interchangeably.

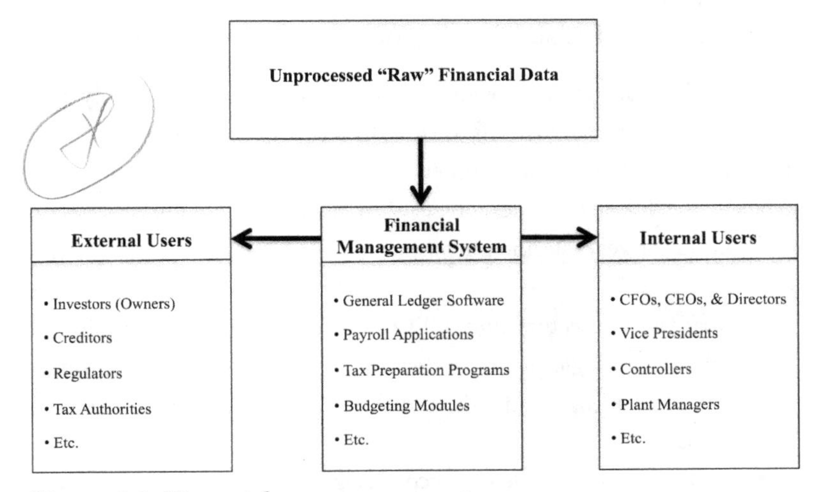

Figure 1.1 Financial management systems

purchase orders, insurance policies, and lease contracts. Financial management systems convert raw financial data into relevant and reliable information useful to external and internal decision makers.

Financial management systems are composed of numerous modules and reporting applications unique to the environments in which they function; however, common to all financial information systems is *general ledger software*. General ledger software is used to record economic events, accumulate activities in specific accounts, analyze accounts receivable, manage payments to creditors, track inventory, maintain depreciation schedules, and streamline financial reporting processes.

Most financial management systems also include payroll software for distributing paychecks, transferring withholdings to tax authorities, and performing the year-end filings of required IRS forms, such as W-2s and 1099s. Other components may include cost accounting software, budgeting applications, simulation packages, and forecasting modules. Functioning as an integrated set of specialized subroutines, these components convert raw data into uniquely formatted reports for dissemination to a diverse group of stakeholders and decision makers.

As Figure 1.1 illustrates, the users of accounting information are both internal and external to the reporting entity. The needs and characteristics of each user group are discussed next.

Internal Users of Accounting Information

Accounting information provided to internal users can be highly confidential and company-specific. Thus, internal accounting reports are often custom-designed and uniquely tailored for specific user groups. For instance, the following internal decision makers rely upon accounting information for very specific purposes:

- Boards of directors and CEOs use accounting information to support strategic planning decisions, such as acquiring subsidiaries, distributing dividends, and shifting manufacturing operations abroad.
- Treasurers and CFOs use accounting information to make financial management decisions, such as investing excess cash reserves, determining annual bonuses, and financing expansion with debt or with equity.
- Controllers use accounting information to analyze cost behaviors, to measure operating efficiency, and to determine breakeven points.
- Human resources officers use accounting information to make hiring decisions, to measure health care costs, and to forecast retirement fund requirements.
- Engineers and researchers use accounting information to estimate the cost of improving quality, to measure manufacturing efficiency, and to prepare budgets supporting the R&D pipeline.
- Marketing and sales managers use accounting information to forecast sales, to make product mix decisions, and to support brand management decisions.

The second half of this book is devoted entirely to the use of accounting information by internal decision makers. Chapter 5 discusses *long-term* forecasting, whereas Chapter 6 addresses *short-term* forecasting and operational budgeting. Chapter 7 examines cost behavior and its impact on profitability, and Chapter 8 focuses on the importance of accounting information for evaluating capital investment decisions. The remaining portion of this chapter and the three chapters that follow pertain to accounting information used by *external* decision makers, in particular the investors and creditors of publicly owned, for-profit corporations.

External Users of Accounting Information

Investors and creditors are generally considered the *primary* external users of accounting information. Other external users include regulatory bodies (such as the Federal Trade Commission and the Public Utilities Commission), tax authorities (including the Internal Revenue Service and the Social Security Administration), and a host of other stakeholders with vested interests in the financial affairs of a particular business entity (common examples include labor unions, suppliers, and customers).

Investors (Shareholders)

Investors are the *owners* of for-profit corporations. Many privately owned corporations are so small that there is no separation between owners and management—in other words, they are one and the same. Publicly owned corporations can have millions of external shareholders, few of whom actually take part in managing the daily operations of the company whose shares they own. Thus, in publicly owned corporations, a separation exists between owners and managers.[3] The shareholders of these corporations are on the outside looking in, and they depend heavily upon financial accounting information to keep them informed.

Existing and potential investors require a basic level of financial literacy in order for accounting information to be useful to them. As their financial literacy improves, so does their ability to measure their return on investment, compare performances among competing firms in the same industry, and assess whether a company will continue as a going concern. Perhaps most importantly, financial literacy enables investors to formulate sensible valuations of stock prices and to become more adept at predicting changes in investment values over time.

[3]Managers are often shareholders of the corporations for whom they work; however, the vast majority of a corporation's shareholders are typically not its employees.

Creditors (Lenders)

Unlike investors, *creditors* rarely have an ownership stake in publicly owned corporations. As the term implies, creditors extend *credit* to companies with an expectation of being repaid and they are often compensated with *interest* for doing so. Creditors include bankers, bondholders, suppliers, venture capitalists, and numerous other providers of debt financing.

Creditors rely heavily upon financial accounting information to evaluate the credit risk associated with a borrower's likelihood of default. As such, they are especially interested in a borrower's ability to generate enough cash flow to satisfy debt service obligations over the term of a loan agreement. High-credit-risk borrowers are charged higher rates of interest than low-credit-risk borrowers.

Investors and creditors both rely upon accounting reports to assess the amount, the timing, and the uncertainty associated with a company's future cash flows.[4] Given the importance of accounting information to both user groups, it is important that access to reliable information be readily available. The remainder of this chapter discusses the financial reporting requirements of publicly owned corporations and the integrity of the information that they provide.

Reporting Requirements of Publicly Owned Corporations

Publicly owned corporations are those whose stock is listed and traded on organized exchanges, such as the New York Stock Exchange (NYSE) and the National Association of Securities Dealers Automated Quotations (NASDAQ). The Securities and Exchange Commission (SEC) mandates by law that all publicly owned corporations make information freely available to everyone, including investors and creditors. The *EDGAR* link on the SEC website (www.sec.gov) provides open access to more than 20 million filings submitted by publicly owned entities. These enterprises are required to submit dozens of reports to the SEC on a regular basis. Of these reports, two are of primary importance to this book—the *10-Q*

[4]Being able to assess the amounts, timing, and risk associated with future cash flows enables investors and creditors to set realistic expectations about their potential returns.

and the *10-K.* The 10-Q is a required *quarterly* report, whereas the 10-K is a much longer and more detailed *annual* report. Both provide valuable information about a corporation's products, markets, employees, executive competition packages, and risk factors.[5]

At the heart of every 10-Q and 10-K is a rather lengthy section devoted to financial accounting and financial reporting. It is in this section that a corporation's *general purpose financial statements* are presented. These statements typically include comparative balance sheets, income statements, statements of cash flows, and statements of retained earnings.[6] Each of these reports is discussed in detail throughout this book. For now it is important to be aware of two things. First, they are called *general purpose* financial statements because their structure and content are somewhat generic and boilerplate across all reporting entities—in short, they provide *a one size fits all* function. Second, each statement has a unique purpose that makes it useful to investors, creditors, and other decision makers in assessing the amount, timing, and uncertainty of future cash flows.

A balance sheet reveals a corporation's financial position at a point in time, meaning that it reports the resources of an entity (its assets), and the claims to those resources by investors and creditors, at a *specific date.* An income statement reports a corporation's results of operations over a *period of time*—most often one quarter or one year. In essence, it reveals a

---

[5]Many corporations also publish annual reports in hardcopy and/or digital formats. These reports are similar in content to the 10-K reports filed with the SEC; however, unlike the 10-Ks, they are usually full-color documents filled with glossy photographs featuring executives, manufacturing facilities, smiling customers, and other nonfinancial images. Their flashy designs have attracted criticism by some who contend they have evolved from being financial documents used primarily by investors and creditors, to being glitzy *public relations materials* used by a diverse audience for multiple purposes. Annual reports are not filed with the SEC; rather, they are sent directly by a corporation to interested parties that request them.

[6]General purpose financial statements are often referred to by alternative names. For instance, balance sheets can be called *statements of financial position,* whereas income statements can be called *earnings statements* or *statements of operations.* Also, many corporations provide a more detailed *statement of shareholders' equity* instead of the simpler statement of retained earnings, and most corporations include a separate *statement of comprehensive income* among their general purpose financial reports.

corporation's net income (its revenues less its expenses) *between* two balance sheet dates. A statement of cash flows reconciles a company's cash balance at the beginning of the period with its cash balance at the end of the period. It does so by classifying sources and uses of cash into three types of business activities (operating activities, investing activities, and financing activities). Finally, a statement of retained earnings reveals periodic increases in a corporation's equity attributed to being profitable, as well as periodic decreases in equity attributed to being unprofitable and/or to declaring dividends. Equity simply refers to the *ownership claims* of shareholders. Distinctions among the various financial statements will be discussed in greater detail throughout Chapters 2 through 4.

Generally Accepted Accounting Principles

It is essential that the accounting information presented in general purpose financial statements is consistent with a conceptual framework and comparable across reporting entities. To that end, publicly owned corporations must adhere to a formal set of standards, concepts, and practices that guide the preparation of the financial statements provided to investors, creditors, and other external stakeholders.

In the United States, these standards, concepts, and practices are commonly referred to as generally accepted accounting principles (GAAP), and since 1973, the rule-making body sanctioned by the SEC to create, guide, and promulgate GAAP has been the Financial Accounting Standards Board (FASB). Other boards and committees preceded the SEC's formation of the FASB, but for a variety of reasons, they no longer exist.[7]

[7]Accounting principles and standards vary by country. For instance, member countries of the European Union (and many others, as well) comply with standards, concepts, and practices established by the International Accounting Standards Board (IASB). The IASB is responsible for issuing International Financial Reporting Standards (IFRS). In response to an expanding global economy and to the growth of international capital markets, the London-based IASB has played a key role in attempting to harmonize accounting practices around the world. In particular, it has strived to improve the uniformity between US GAAP and IFRS. To date, a complex web of legal, economic, and philosophical obstacles impedes a convergence to a single set of global accounting standards; however, progress toward that end is being made.

The FASB is a private not-for-profit organization. Its seven full-time members—with the support of the SEC—are largely responsible for establishing an evolving body of reporting standards and for making continuous improvements to the overall usefulness of financial accounting information. The private sector status of the FASB prevents it from having any legal authority to enforce GAAP; however, failure by a publicly owned corporation to comply with GAAP can subject both it and its executive officers to legal prosecution.

Financial Statement Integrity

Investors, creditors, and other external users of general purpose financial statements need assurance that the accounting information in these reports has been prepared in compliance with GAAP. Moreover, they have to be confident that the financial statements are free of material misstatements and represent fairly the financial activities of the reporting entity. To that end, the annual financial statements issued by all publicly owned corporations must be audited by licensed Certified Public Accountants (CPAs).[8]

Audits and Assurance

In their capacity as auditors, CPAs serve the public interest as independent third-party watchdogs responsible for providing *reasonable assurance* that a company's financial statements are prepared in compliance with GAAP. It is their responsibility to render an opinion whether financial statements are reliable, complete, and fair representations of a company's financial position, results of operations, and cash flow activities. As part of the audit process, CPAs conduct in-depth interviews with key members of a company's management, evaluate the soundness of a company's internal control systems, perform bank reconciliations, and statistically sample key accounts (such as inventory and accounts receivable) to ascertain whether their balances appear valid.

[8]Many of the largest publicly owned corporations listed on the NYSE and NASDAQ exchanges are audited by one of four accounting firms. These giant international firms—referred to collectively as *The Big 4*—are Deloitte, EY, PwC, and KPMG.

Audits play a critical role in maintaining financial reporting integrity. Yet, they are not 100 percent foolproof. Highly publicized business failures in recent years have given rise to questions concerning audit effectiveness and auditor independence. Although CPAs are entrusted to perform audits on behalf of the general public, the companies that they audit hire and pay them. Many believe that this arrangement compromises an auditor's independence and creates potential for *the fox guarding the henhouse.* Other criticisms of auditor independence have arisen from CPA firms providing consulting and advisory services to their clients. As consultants and advisers, CPA firms clearly become their clients' *advocates.*

Governmental Intervention

Congress passed the Sarbanes–Oxley Act (SOX) in 2002, shortly after the collapse of Enron. In addition to limiting the scope of consulting and advisory services that CPA firms can provide to audit clients, SOX requires CPAs to issue separate reports on the effectiveness of their clients' systems of internal control. Moreover, SOX legislation holds CEOs and CFOs of publicly owned corporations *personally* responsible for certifying the fairness of their company's financial statements. SOX legislation also resulted in the creation of the Public Company Accounting Oversight Board (PCAOB), which has the power to monitor the quality of audits conducted by public accounting firms and to administer penalties for substandard audits or malfeasance.

SOX and the creation of the PCAOB have made significant strides in restoring the confidence that external decision makers have in the financial reporting processes; nevertheless, there remains much room for improvement. It is important to emphasize that financial statement users have a responsibility to be financially literate and to exercise caution, due diligence, and sound judgment when making investment decisions.

Summary

Accounting has been discussed throughout this chapter in the context of a financial management system, the purpose of which is to transform unprocessed financial data into reports used by internal and external decision makers. Internal accounting reports are custom-designed and uniquely tailored for specific user groups. External accounting information is disseminated in the form of general purpose financial statements.

The SEC, the FASB, and CPAs play important roles in maintaining the integrity of general purpose financial statements issued to external users by publicly owned corporations. The structure and use of these statements will be examined in Chapters 2 through 4. Chapters 5 through 8 are devoted to managerial issues and the internal use of accounting information.

CHAPTER 2

Corporate Financial Statements

Four general purpose financial statements issued by publicly owned corporations were identified in Chapter 1: balance sheet, income statement, statement of cash flows, and statement of retained earnings. This chapter revisits these publicly available reports in greater detail.

The Balance Sheet

The balance sheet is a *snapshot* of a corporation's *financial position* at a specific point in time. In fact, balance sheets are often referred to as statements of financial position. A corporation's financial position refers to its assets and the claims to those assets by creditors and shareholders. A balance sheet is aptly named, because the relationship among its elements can be expressed as a rudimentary formula referred to as the *accounting equation*. The accounting equation simply states that the assets of a corporation equal the sum of its liabilities and shareholders' equity (A = L + E).

Figure 2.1 provides a simple and straightforward illustration of a corporate balance sheet.[1] Notice that Weston's total assets of $1,000,000 equal the sum of its liabilities ($360,000) plus its shareholders' equity ($640,000). As expected, the underlying accounting equation (A = L + E) is in balance ($1,000,000 = $360,000 + $640,000).

The heading of Weston's balance sheet states that all figures are in *thousands* of dollars. Thus, the reported cash figure of $24,000 actually

[1]To streamline this illustration, the Figure 2.1 balance sheet reveals Weston's financial position on December 31 of the *current year only*. Financial statements actually issued by publicly owned corporations are *comparative*, meaning that they provide several columns of financial information corresponding to multiple years.

Balance Sheet
Weston Corporation
December 31, Current Year
(All Figures in Thousands of Dollars)

Assets	
Current Assets	
Cash	$ 24,000
Accounts Receivable (at NRV)	86,000
Inventory	108,000
Prepaid Items	2,000
Total Current Assets	$ 220,000
Noncurrent Assets	
Buildings & Equipment (at NBV)	$ 700,000
Land	80,000
Total Assets	$1,000,000
Liabilities	
Current Liabilities	
Trade Accounts Payable	$ 98,000
Accrued Expenses	12,000
Total Current Liabilities	$ 110,000
Noncurrent Liabilities	
Long-Term Notes Payable	250,000
Total Liabilities	$ 360,000
Shareholders' Equity	
Common Stock (no par value)	$ 150,000
Retained Earnings	490,000
Total Shareholders' Equity	$ 640,000
Total Liabilities & Shareholders' Equity	$1,000,000

Figure 2.1 The balance sheet

means that the company's cash balance is approximately *$24 million*; likewise, the $1,000,000 total asset figure denotes total resources of approximately *$1 billion.* This form of restatement is common practice in financial reporting. In fact, some publicly owned corporations are so large that they restate their financial statements in *millions* of dollars.

The individual elements of a corporate balance sheet—assets, liabilities, and shareholders' equity—are identified and discussed in the following sections. All references pertaining to specific amounts reported in Figure 2.1 will remain stated in thousands of dollars. For instance, all references to the company's cash will be stated as $24,000, not $24 million.

Assets

Assets reported in a balance sheet are defined as *economic resources expected to bring future benefit*. Economic resources are those that can be measured and quantified in *monetary terms*.[2] Future benefit refers to the potential of assets to support and to make possible the generation of future cash flow. Weston's balance sheet in Figure 2.1 reveals two asset classifications: *Current Assets* and *Noncurrent Assets*. Both classifications are composed of economic resources expected to bring future benefit. What distinguishes current assets from noncurrent assets is how *quickly* their benefits are expected, and the *type* of benefits they provide.

Current Assets

Current assets are economic resources expected to provide benefits in one year, or in one operating cycle, whichever is *longer*. With relatively few exceptions, one year is generally longer than one operating cycle for most companies.[3] Thus, current assets are usually expected to provide benefits in *one year or less*. The primary benefit that current assets provide is a continuous source of *cash flow* to satisfy recurring obligations incurred in

---

[2]By restricting the assets reported in a balance sheet to economic resources, the value of indispensable *human resources* is omitted. The subjectivity and difficulty associated with measuring the monetary value of human capital preclude its direct inclusion in the financial statements.

[3]An *operating cycle* is the average time that elapses from when a business invests cash in inventory, sells that inventory to customers, and eventually collects the cash owed from those customers. For most retailers, wholesalers, and manufacturers, the time required to complete this cycle is significantly less than one year. Thus, current assets are generally considered those resources whose benefits will be realized in *one year or less*. Operating cycles and their measurement are discussed in Chapter 4.

daily operations (e.g., acquiring inventory, paying utilities, buying insurance, compensating employees, etc.).

Current assets are listed in the order of *liquidity*—which means how quickly they are expected to convert into cash. Cash is always listed first, because it is immediately available to satisfy outstanding obligations. Weston's balance sheet in Figure 2.1 lists accounts receivable (from credit sales made to customers) second, and inventory third. Accounts receivable is considered more liquid than inventory because inventory sold to credit customers does not provide an immediate source of cash flow. Instead, inventory sold on credit is exchanged for accounts receivable, which subsequently convert to cash when collected. The prepaid items shown in Weston's balance sheet are its *least* liquid current asset. Prepayments are a topic discussed in Chapter 3.

The critical role current assets play in providing sources of continuous cash flow makes them especially important to investors and creditors.[4] Thus, downward adjustments to current asset values are sometimes warranted to reflect declines in their future cash flow potential. For instance, Weston's $86,000 accounts receivable shown in Figure 2.1 is reported at *net realizable value* (NRV). This means that Weston's credit customers actually owe an amount *in excess* of $86,000; however, management believes that some of these accounts may not be collectible. Thus, Weston's $86,000 (NRV) figure is an *estimate* of management's most reasonable expectation of how much cash will eventually be collected. Although this estimate is somewhat subjective, it is considered more relevant to the external users of the company's financial statements than the total dollar amount of accounts receivable actually outstanding.[5]

Noncurrent Assets

Noncurrent assets take much longer than current assets to provide benefits. Their benefits often span many years or decades. Unlike most current

---

[4]The importance that investors and creditors place on the cash-generating potential of current assets is a Chapter 4 topic. Here, it suffices to say that cash flow is important to investors and creditors because it impacts a company's stock prices, its dividend policies, and its ability to satisfy debt obligations.

[5]Other current assets subject to valuation write-downs include investment portfolios that have lost value due to declining market prices and inventory items that have lost value due to damage, spoilage, or technological obsolescence.

assets, noncurrent assets are not generally intended to provide direct sources of cash flow; instead, their primary benefit is the *long-term support* of cash-generating activities.

Weston's balance sheet in Figure 2.1 reports noncurrent assets of buildings, equipment, and land. These assets are not expected to provide direct sources of cash flow because they are not currently *for sale*. Nevertheless, they provide a long-term infrastructure necessary to showcase inventory, sell products, and process customer accounts. Thus, these *tangible* noncurrent assets derive their value by indirectly supporting a company's ability to generate future cash flow.[6]

It is important to realize that noncurrent assets such as land, buildings, and equipment are most often reported in the balance sheet at amounts based on their *original acquisition costs*, not their current *fair market values*. For instance, Weston's balance sheet in Figure 2.1 reports land that was initially acquired for $80,000; however, its current fair market value could actually be much higher. Reporting noncurrent assets on the basis of their acquisition costs is a fundamental tenet of generally accepted accounting principles (U.S. GAAP) referred to as the *historical cost convention*. The rationale for this controversial principle is that determining the *actual value* of noncurrent assets can be extremely *subjective*. Thus, given that most noncurrent assets will not be sold in the foreseeable future, proponents of the historical cost convention argue that it is better to report them at objectively determinable acquisition costs than at subjective estimates of their fair market values.[7]

---

[6] *Tangible* noncurrent assets are those having an actual *physical substance*, such as manufacturing equipment, buildings, vehicles, and land. These assets are commonly called *fixed assets*. Balance sheets also may include noncurrent assets that are *intangible*, such as patents, copyrights, and goodwill. Noncurrent assets can also be *financial instruments* held as long-term investments. The coverage of intangible assets and long-term investments is beyond the scope of this book.

[7] U.S. GAAP makes an exception to the historical cost convention when the future benefit potential of a noncurrent asset becomes *significantly impaired*. For example, assume that the discovery of groundwater pollution impairs the use of a land causing its estimated market value to decline significantly below its acquisition cost. In this situation, the land would be reported in the balance sheet at its more subjective estimated fair market value instead of its more objective historical cost. International Financial Reporting Standards do not adhere to the historical cost principle.

Finally, it is important to note that the buildings and equipment shown in Figure 2.1 are reported at a net book value (NBV) of $700,000. Although this figure is based upon the historical costs of these assets, their initial acquisition costs actually were *in excess* of $700,000. This topic is discussed more fully in Chapter 3; however, at this point, a simple explanation is warranted.

When a noncurrent asset (other than land) is first acquired, the cost of the asset is divided by its estimated years of useful life to determine the amount by which its NBV must be *reduced* each year in the balance sheet.[8] For instance, assume that a business purchased a truck for $80,000 at the beginning of the year and at that time management estimated its useful life to be 8 years. At the end of each year, the truck's NBV reported in the balance sheet will be reduced by $10,000 ($80,000 ÷ 8 years = $10,000 per year). Thus, after 8 years, its NBV will be zero.

The process described above is referred to as *depreciation*. Depreciation is *not* an attempt to measure wear-and-tear, technological obsolescence, or the decline of an asset's fair market value. It is simply a systematic way to take into account the ongoing expiration of an asset's future benefit potential with the passage of time. All tangible noncurrent assets other than land undergo this process. Land has an *unlimited* useful life, so its future benefit potential does not expire with the passage of time. As such, the historical cost of land reported in the balance sheet is not reduced systematically from year to year.

Liabilities

Liabilities are generally defined as *economic obligations that require the future use of assets in settlement*. Economic obligations arise from transactions that can be measured in monetary terms. In most instances, cash is the asset used to settle these obligations.[9]

---

[8]An estimated residual (salvage) value is often subtracted from the asset's acquisition cost before dividing by its estimated useful life; however, the general concept described here is the same.

[9]Liabilities are sometimes settled by delivering goods or services to customers. This form of settlement is discussed in Chapter 3.

Weston's balance sheet in Figure 2.1 reveals two liability classifications: *Current Liabilities* and *Noncurrent Liabilities*. Both classifications are composed of economic obligations that require future settlement. What distinguishes current liabilities from noncurrent liabilities is *when* their settlement is due.

Current Liabilities

Current liabilities are obligations requiring settlement within one year, or one operating cycle, whichever is *longer*. Thus, they require settlement in the same time frame that current assets covert into cash. For reasons discussed previously, this means that current liabilities generally require settlement in *one year or less*. A company's survival often hinges upon its current assets being capable of providing enough cash inflow to settle its current liabilities as they come due.

Weston's balance sheet in Figure 2.1 lists two current liabilities: trade accounts payable and other accrued liabilities. Trade accounts payable are obligations that a company owes to its suppliers for credit purchases of *inventory*. Trade accounts payable are often a company's largest current liability. This is certainly true in Weston's balance sheet, which reports a $98,000 obligation to its inventory vendors. Weston's only other current liability—other accrued liabilities—represents a combination of miscellaneous obligations other than those arising from inventory purchases. These unpaid obligations often include wages owed to employees, income taxes owed to the IRS, and interest owed to banks and other creditors. In Weston's case, these obligations total $12,000. Had any of them been considered *material* in amount, they would be listed separately in the balance sheet with designations such as salaries payable, taxes payable, or interest payable.[10] Determining the threshold of materiality is a subjective process requiring a great deal of judgment.

[10]In financial reporting, the threshold of *materiality* refers to amounts so large that they have the potential to influence interpretations and decisions made by financial statement users. In Figure 2.1, the $12,000 other accrued liabilities figure is considered material *in total*; however, none of the obligations included in this figure is considered material *individually*. As such, they are not reported separately.

Noncurrent Liabilities

Noncurrent liabilities have settlement dates or maturity dates that often extend many years into the future. Unlike most current liabilities, noncurrent liabilities are backed by formal written contacts, including mortgage bonds, debenture bonds, and long-term notes payable. Most noncurrent liability contracts require scheduled debt service payments until the obligations are fully settled. For instance, a 10-year note payable owed to a bank might involve a series of 120 monthly payments.[11] Those payments coming due in the near future—usually within one year—are reported as current liabilities in the balance sheet, designated as *the current portion of long-term debt.*

Weston's balance sheet in Figure 2.1 reports only one noncurrent obligation—a $250,000 note payable. This obligation most likely arose from a decision to finance some of its noncurrent assets with debt. Later in this chapter, an examination of Weston's statement of cash flows will reveal whether any long-term borrowing activity occurred in the current period.

Shareholders' Equity

A simple two-word definition of shareholders' equity is *shareholder ownership*. After subtracting from total assets all of a corporation's obligations, what remains are ownership claims belonging to shareholders (A − L = E). These ownership claims stem from two sources: *contributions* from shareholders in exchange for shares of stock, and *profits* earned by the corporation that are retained and reinvested. The former is generally referred to as *paid-in capital* (or *contributed capital*), whereas the latter is referred to as *retained earnings*.

Paid-in Capital

Shareholder claims to assets arising from their capital contributions appear in the shareholders' equity section of a balance sheet as *common stock*. All for-profit corporations raise capital by selling shares of stock to investors,

[11] In addition to reducing the principal amount of the outstanding loan balance, debt service payments typically include interest charges, as well.

and common stock is the most basic classification of stock that is issued.[12] Common shares give investors voting rights in proportion to the number of shares they own—meaning that the more shares individual investors own, the more influence and control they have in determining who will be elected to the corporation's board of directors. Thus, common stock ownership enables investors to have a voice in strategic decision making.

In the United States, corporations come into existence by obtaining a *corporate charter* from a particular state. A company does not have to conduct activities or maintain a physical presence in its state of incorporation. Nevertheless, it must abide by the regulatory laws of that state. Thus, the decision to incorporate in a particular state is based largely upon its regulatory flexibility and leniency. Delaware and Nevada attract many businesses to incorporate there for this reason.

Weston's balance sheet in Figure 2.1 reports common stock of $150,000. Assuming that Weston is a publicly owned corporation, this figure is the total capital contributed by investors in exchange for common stock issued through initial public offerings (IPOs).[13] Note that Weston's common stock is designated as having *no par value*. Some states require that corporations establish a legal floor beneath which the price per share of an IPO must not fall. This minimum issue price is referred to as *par value*.[14] If Weston were incorporated in a state that required par values, its common stock would be reported in the balance sheet using *two separate lines* instead of one. The first line would report the *total par value* raised by selling stock to investors (the par value per share times the number of shares issued). The second line would report the amount received from investors *in excess* of total par value. Together, the sum of the two lines would equal the $150,000 figure shown in Figure 2.1.

---

[12]Some corporations also offer investors a classification called *preferred stock;* however, most corporations offer only common shares. If a corporation offers only one type of stock, it is required that its classification be common stock.

[13]Publicly owned corporations do not sell shares of stock *directly* to investors. Instead, they engage the services of investment bankers to make their shares widely available to brokers and other interested parties.

[14]Par values per share are generally set at extremely low amounts—often fractions of a cent. As such, they are of little significance and many states no longer require them.

Retained Earnings

Unlike paid-in capital (which represents equity claims to assets from shareholder investment in common stock), retained earnings are shareholder claims to assets resulting from the retention of corporate *profits* to finance growth and expansion. The fruits of this good fortune belong to the shareholders—after all, as owners they have equity claims to what the corporation earns. The alternative to retaining profit is to distribute it to shareholders as *dividends*. The board of directors sets dividend policy and determines the amount of profit to be distributed as dividends and the amount to be retained for financing growth.

Weston's balance sheet in Figure 2.1 reports retained earnings of $490,000. This figure represents total profits earned by the company over its entire existence, less any dividends declared since it was first incorporated.[15] In theory, this amount represents undistributed assets *potentially* available to Weston's shareholders as dividends. Yet, an examination of Weston's assets reveals cash of only $24,000, which is significantly less than the $490,000 retained earnings figure. This is not an unusual situation given that the amount of cash that a company has in its possession is not equivalent to the earnings it has retained since its inception.

The differences between cash flow and earnings will be examined more completely in Chapter 3. At this point, it is time to shift the discussion away from the balance sheet and focus upon the *income statement.*

The Income Statement

Income statements—sometimes called earnings statements or statements of operations—report an enterprise's *results of operations* for a *period of time* (often one year or one quarter). Conceptually—in its most basic form—an income statement can be expressed as an equation in which net income is the difference between *revenue* and *expenses* (Revenue − Expenses = Net Income).[16] As discussed previously, net income increases

[15]Certain events other than income and dividend activities have the potential to influence retained earnings and/or a shareholders' equity account called accumulated other comprehensive income. These events are beyond the scope of this book.

[16]When expenses *exceed* revenue, the difference is referred to as a *net loss.*

retained earnings in the shareholders' equity section of a corporation's balance sheet.

Revenue

Revenues, often referred to as *net sales*, are increases in assets that result from providing goods and services to customers for a profit. Corporations earn the increases in assets that result from their profit-related activities; so in effect, these assets belong to the shareholders of the corporation. Thus, revenue also may be viewed as increases in shareholders' equity resulting from profit-related activities. This makes sense, given that earning revenue increases net income, and net income increases retained earnings in the shareholders' equity section of the balance sheet.

The timing of *when* revenue should be reported in the income statement is not always clear-cut.[17] In most situations, however, revenue should be reported in the income statement whenever all of the following conditions have been met:

- A contract has been established between the seller and the customer.
- The seller's obligations are clearly identified and stipulated.
- The total contract price is measurable and capable of being allocated to the seller's specific obligations.
- The seller's obligation has been satisfied, thereby completing the earnings process.

The first three conditions are satisfied when a seller and a customer mutually agree upon the measurable terms of a sale—such as the delivery of 5,000 gallons of diesel fuel at $4.00 per gallon by a specific date. The earnings process is considered complete when the seller has provided the goods or services in accordance with agreed upon terms.[18] Once the first

[17]Complex measurement and reporting issues are associated with revenue from long-term installment sales contracts and from multiyear construction projects.

[18]If a contract specifies multiple obligations, a portion of the total selling price is allocated to each obligation, and revenue is recognized as each obligation of the contract is satisfied. Contracts can be formal written agreements or less formal verbal agreements.

Income Statement Weston Corporation For the Period Ending December 31, Current Year (In Thousands)	
Net Sales	$960,000
Cost of Goods Sold	384,000
Gross Profit	576,000
Selling, General, & Administrative Expenses	357,000
Income Before Interest & Income Taxes	$219,000
Interest Expense	20,000
Income Tax Expense	79,000
Net Income	$120,000

Figure 2.2 The income statement

two conditions are met, revenue should be reported in the income statement even if a full cash settlement has not been received, so long as the likelihood of it being received is high. Such is the case in nearly all sales made to credit customers.

Weston's income statement in Figure 2.2 reports net sales of $960,000. *Net sales* refers to revenue earned by a business net of any discounts or allowances. Consistent with Weston's balance sheet, all of the amounts in the income statement are reported in *thousands* of dollars. Thus, Weston's net sales in the current year were actually $960 million.

The $960,000 net sales figure is *revenue* that Weston *earned* in the current year. This figure does *not* equate to the amount of cash it received from customers. As previously discussed, Weston's balance sheet in Figure 2.1 reports accounts receivable of $86,000, indicating that a portion of its revenue is from credit sales to customers. Differences between cash received from customers and revenue reported in the income statement are examined more closely in Chapter 3.

Expenses

There is no such thing as a free lunch, and there is no such thing as *free revenue*—all revenue comes at a *cost*. To that end, *expenses represent the cost of resources consumed to generate revenue.* Expenses decrease net income reported in the income statement; so in effect, they also *decrease retained earnings* reported in the shareholders' equity section of the balance sheet. This makes sense, given that shareholder claims to assets decrease as resources are consumed.

Expenses reported in the income statement arise from a very important tenet of financial accounting called the *matching principle.* The matching principle requires that income statements *match* the cost of resources consumed with revenue earned. Matching the cost of resources consumed with revenue earned is sometimes straightforward and objective; other times it is not. In many cases the matching process is rather arbitrary. This makes the measurement of net income for a specific reporting period a rather arbitrary process as well.

To illustrate, assume that a bakery sells bread to grocery stores using a delivery truck. To generate revenue, the bakery must incur certain expenses by consuming resources. In any particular year, several truck-related costs matched with revenue are easy to measure objectively. Examples include the truck's insurance, fuel, and maintenance expenses, as well as the truck driver's annual salary expense. But what about the bakery's initial cost of acquiring the truck? The truck is a noncurrent asset that supports revenue generation for many years. Accordingly, a portion of its acquisition cost is *matched* with revenue each year over its useful life and its NBV reported in the balance sheet declines by an equal amount. This describes the depreciation process discussed previously. The amount of the truck's acquisition cost matched each year with revenue reported in the income statement is referred to as *depreciation expense.*

If the bakery purchased the truck for $80,000, and estimated its useful life as 8 years, the income statement would report an annual depreciation expense of $10,000 ($80,000 ÷ 8 years = $10,000 per year). Likewise, the truck's NBV reported in the balance sheet would decrease each year by $10,000.[19] In essence, depreciation enables a portion of a noncurrent

[19]Notice that the truck's NPV shown in the balance sheet at the end of each year equals its initial acquisition cost less its *accumulated* depreciation for the number of years it has been in service. Thus, after 3 years of service, the truck's NBV would be $50,000 (its $80,000 historical cost, less 3 years of accumulated depreciation at $10,000 per year). The process of depreciation will be revisited in Chapter 3.

asset's cost to be *matched* with revenue in the income statement and its NBV to be reduced in the balance sheet, signifying an ongoing *expiration* of its future benefit potential. The process keeps the accounting equation (A = L + E) in balance by reducing assets each year by the same amount that retained earnings is reduced in shareholders' equity. In this simple illustration, the depreciation process reduces assets and equity by $10,000 each year.

Weston's income statement in Figure 2.2 reports several expense and cost classifications. The $384,000 *cost of goods sold* figure represents the cost of Weston's inventory that was *matched* with current year net sales. Cost of goods sold is referred to as a product cost because it matches the cost to acquire inventory (products) directly with revenue generated from selling it. Weston's $384,000 cost of goods sold is matched with net sales of $960,000, resulting in a *gross profit* for the year of $576,000. The importance of measuring gross profit is discussed at length in Chapter 4.

The *selling, general, and administrative* (SG&A) *expenses* of $357,000 in Weston's income statement are considered *period costs* because unlike *product costs*, they correspond to the *time period* in which revenue was generated, not to products that were sold. Weston's current year SG&A costs may include:

- Marketing and promotion costs;
- Postage and shipping costs;
- Utility costs, such as electricity and natural gas;
- Administrative salaries and wages;
- Professional costs, such as legal and accounting fees;
- Travel costs;
- Office costs, such as telephone, Internet service, and printing costs;
- Depreciation expense associated with noncurrent assets, such as delivery trucks.

Weston's income statement in Figure 2.2 separately reports interest expense of $20,000 and income tax expense of $79,000. The reason for listing these expenses as separate line items is discussed in Chapter 4. For now, it is important to recognize that the $20,000 interest expense relates to the $250,000 long-term note payable reported in the company's balance sheet in Figure 2.1.

Weston's *net income* figure of $120,000 is the *bottom line* measure of its results of operations for the current year.[20] Any undistributed assets associated with this figure belong to Weston's shareholders. The total claims to undistributed assets related to earnings are reported in shareholders' equity of the balance sheet as retained earnings.

The Statement of Retained Earnings

The statement of retained earnings ties together retained earnings reported in shareholders' equity at the beginning of the year with retained earnings reported in shareholders' equity at the end of the year. Corporations expand in size as they generate profit, causing both their assets and their retained earnings increase. Any distributions of profit to shareholders as dividends cause both assets and retained earnings to decrease. Thus, the statement of retained earnings reports the *net* amount by which a corporation's assets and retained earnings increase each year from the earnings it retains.[21] As noted in Chapter 1, many corporations provide a more detailed *statement of shareholders' equity* instead of the simpler statement of retained earnings.

Figure 2.3 illustrates how profits reported in the income statement flow through the statement of retained earnings and onto the balance sheet. These linkages are referred to as financial statement *integration.*

The financial statement integration diagramed in Figure 2.3 illustrates that net income reported in the income statement directly increases

[20]Income statements issued by publicly owned corporations report results of operations for *multiple years* and include *earnings per share* (EPS) figures directly below net income for each year reported. EPS is discussed in Chapter 4. Moreover, corporations are required to include a separate financial statement called the *statement of comprehensive income* to report other revenue and expense items not included in their regular income statements. The accumulation of these other comprehensive income items from year-to-year is reported in the shareholders' equity section of the balance sheet in a similar fashion to the manner in which retained earnings report the accumulation of regular income over time. The topic of other comprehensive income items is beyond the scope of this book.

[21]When a corporation suffers a *net loss*, its statement of retained earnings reports the amount by which assets and retained earnings have *decreased.*

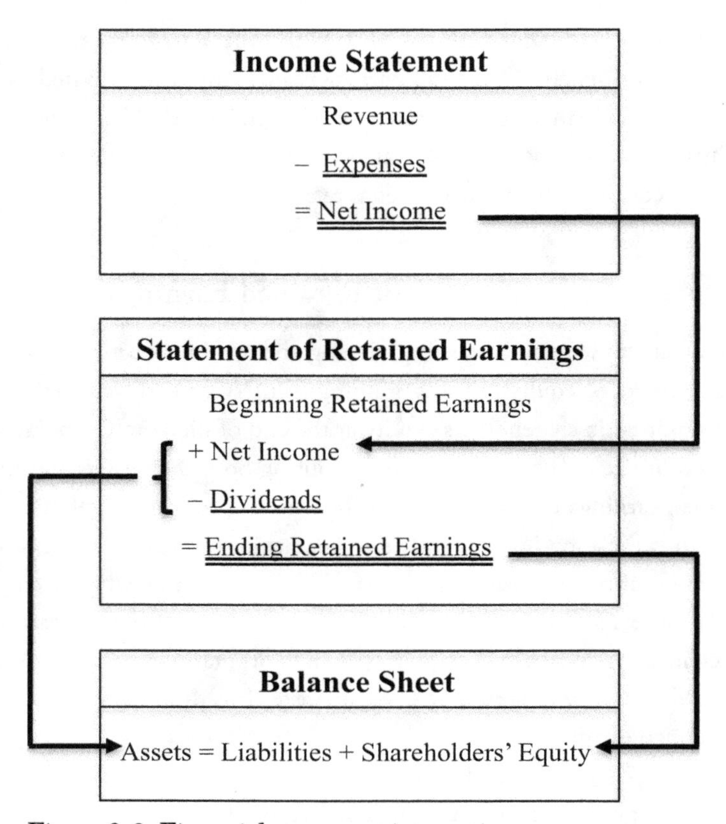

Figure 2.3 Financial statement integration

retained earnings. From the statement of retained earnings flows a *net change* in shareholders' equity that reflects the portion of net income that was distributed as dividends. The net change in shareholders' equity equals the net change in assets that results from the corporation's retention of profits.

Weston's statement of retained earnings in Figure 2.4 shows retained earnings of $385,000 at the beginning of the current year. This was the retained earnings amount reported in its balance sheet at the end of the previous year. The $120,000 net income figure was taken from the corporation's income statement in Figure 2.2. The company's net income, less $15,000 of dividends declared in the current year, is the net increase in Weston's assets and shareholders' equity that resulted from retaining $105,000 of its current year earnings ($120,000 – $15,000 = $105,000).

Statement of Retained Earnings Weston Corporation For the Period Ending December 31, Current Year (In Thousands)	
Beginning Retained Earnings (January 1)	$385,000
Add: Net Income	120,000
Less: Dividends Declared	(15,000)
Ending Retained Earnings (December 31)	$490,000

Figure 2.4 The statement of retained earnings

It is important to realize that publicly owned corporations are not required to pay cash dividends to their shareholders, and many profitable corporations do not.[22] It is not unusual for relatively new corporations to forgo paying dividends and thereby retain their earnings to finance growth. An obligation to pay dividends arises only if the board of directors declares—as a matter of public record—that a distribution of dividends is forthcoming. Once the dividend has been declared, it typically takes 5 to 7 weeks for it to be distributed.

The Statement of Cash Flows

The statement of cash flows reconciles a company's cash reserves at the beginning of a reporting period with the cash reported in its balance sheet at the end of the period. It does so by identifying all of a company's sources and uses of cash during the period that resulted from one of three types of activities: operating activities, investing activities, and financing activities. It is essential to understand how these cash flow activities impact a company's survival.

Weston's statement of cash flows is illustrated in Figure 2.5. Note that cash flows from operating activities are listed first, followed by those from investing activities second, and those from financing activities third. This is the sequence of presentation used by all U.S. Corporations. Weston's

[22]Corporations sometimes issue additional shares of common *stock* to their shareholders in lieu of distributing assets in the form of cash dividends. *Stock dividend* activities are beyond the scope of this book.

Statement of Cash Flows **Weston Corporation** **For the Period Ending December 31, Current Year** **(In Thousands)**	
Cash Flows from Operating Activities	
Cash Received from Customers	$980,000
Cash Paid for Inventory	(410,000)
Cash Paid for Selling, General, & Administrative Expenses	(325,000)
Cash Paid for Interest	(20,000)
Cash Paid for Income Taxes	(80,000)
Net Cash Provided by Operating Activities	$145,000
Cash Flows from Investing Activities	
Cash Proceeds from the Sale of Land	$ 18,000
Cash Paid for the Purchase of Equipment	(190,000)
Net Cash Used for Investing Activities	($172,000)
Cash Flows from Financing Activities	
Cash Proceeds from Issuing Common Stock to Shareholders	$ 50,000
Cash Paid for Dividends	(15,000)
Net Cash Provided by Financing Activities	$ 35,000
Net Increase in Cash from all Activities	$ 8,000
Beginning Cash Balance (January 1)	16,000
Ending Cash Balance (December 31)	$ 24,000

Figure 2.5 The statement of cash flows

$8,000 net increase in cash from all three activities in the current year, added to its $16,000 beginning cash balance on January 1, equals the $24,000 cash amount reported in its Figure 2.1 balance sheet at the end of the year.

Cash Flow from Operating Activities

The operations of an enterprise relate to its ongoing profit-related activities. For this reason, profitability is often referred to as a company's *results of operations*. Thus, cash flows from operating activities are receipts and disbursements of cash related to *generating profit*. Cash received from customers is the primary operating cash inflow for most companies, whereas cash paid for inventory, salaries, taxes, and various administrative costs represent major operating cash outflows. Operating cash flows are a company's *lifeblood of survival*—meaning that to remain a viable going concern its net cash flow provided by operating activities must remain healthy.

Weston's statement of cash flows in Figure 2.5 reports cash received from customers of $980,000.[23] To be consistent with the other financial statements, all amounts are stated in *thousands* of dollars, meaning that Weston actually collected $980 million. Notice that the $980,000 received from customers exceeds by $20,000 the amount of *net sales* reported in the company's Figure 2.2 income statement. The reason for the discrepancy is that revenue earned does not always occur at the same time that cash is collected from customers. In Weston's case, many of its sales are made to credit customers. Thus, $20,000 of what Weston collected from customers in the current year corresponds to credit sales reported in a previous year's income statement.[24]

Weston's operating cash *disbursements* total $835,000, the largest of which are inventory purchases and payments of SG&A costs. Note that total disbursements do not equal the total expenses shown in the company's Figure 2.2 income statement. This is because expenses are not always *incurred* at the same time that cash is disbursed. Reporting differences between the income statement and the statement of cash flows are examined more thoroughly in later chapters. For now, what is important to notice is that Weston's current year operating activities provided a net cash *inflow* of $145,000. This is a favorable indication that the company was able to pay its operating costs as they came due.

Cash Flows from Investing Activities

Unlike operating activities, investing activities do not represent the cash effects of ongoing and recurring revenue and expense transactions.

[23]Weston reports cash flows from operating activities using the *direct method.* In later chapters, an alternative presentation called the *indirect method* will be illustrated.

[24]This resulted in a $20,000 *net decrease* in Weston's *accounts receivable* for the current year.

Instead, they generally refer to buying and selling *noncurrent assets* such as land, buildings, and equipment.[25]

Weston's statement of cash flows in Figure 2.5 shows the cash effects of two investing activities. The first activity (the sale of land) resulted in cash proceeds of $18,000. The second activity (the purchase of equipment) resulted in a cash disbursement of $190,000. Thus, Weston's investing activities resulted in a *negative* cash flow of $172,000 for the year. In contrast to negative net cash flows from operating activities—which can signal financial problems—negative cash flows from investing activities are often indicative of a *strong* financial position. Indeed, vibrant and successful enterprises make frequent investments in plant and equipment as they expand and flourish.

Cash Flows from Financing Activities

Financing activities refer to debt and equity financing transactions. Debt financing activities mostly involve borrowing money and repaying the loans. Equity financing activities often consist of issuing stock to shareholders and paying dividends.[26]

Weston's statement of cash flows in Figure 2.5 shows the cash effects of two financing activities. The first activity (issuing common stock to shareholders) resulted in cash proceeds of $50,000. The second activity (the payment of cash dividends) resulted in a cash disbursement of $15,000. Thus, Weston's financing activities *provided* $35,000 during the year. Both of these transactions are considered equity financing activities, which means that the $250,000 long-term note payable shown in the balance sheet in Figure 2.1 arose from debt financing activities in a *prior year*. Had the $250,000 been borrowed in the current year, the resulting cash proceeds would be shown in the current year statement of cash flows.

Dividends paid to shareholders are considered the *cost* of equity financing. Accordingly, they are classified as *financing activities* in the statement

[25]Investing activities can also involve certain financial assets, such as portfolios of stocks and bonds. They can also include intangible assets, such as patents copyrights, and trademarks.

[26]Other financing activities, such as treasury stock transactions, are commonplace; however, they are beyond the scope of this book.

of cash flows. Interest payments to creditors are a *cost* of debt financing; however, they are classified among the *operating activities* in the statement of cash flows. The reasoning behind this seemingly inconsistent treatment of interest payments is that operating cash flows arise from revenue- and expense activities-associated net income determination. Given that interest expense is a component of net income, interest payments are considered operating cash flows. Dividends are not expenses, so they are not associated with net income determination. Accordingly, dividend payments appear as financing cash flows in the statement of cash flows.

Summary

Publicly owned corporations are required to issue four general purpose financial statements. These statements are primarily for investors and creditors. The balance sheet reports a corporation's financial position. It does so by listing a corporation's assets and claims to those assets by investors and creditors at a specific point in time. The income statement measures a corporation's results of operations (revenues minus expenses) for a period of time. It reports revenue when it is earned and expenses when they are incurred, regardless of when cash is received or paid. The statement of retained earnings reveals how much of a corporation's profits are retained each year and how much are distributed as dividends to investors. The statement of cash flows reports all of a corporation's sources and uses of cash for a period of time. It does so by showing the cash effects of three kinds of activities—operating activities, investing activities, and financing activities.

Chapter 3 examines how relationships among the general purpose financial statements influence the measurement of income. Chapter 4 builds upon these concepts by examining how investors and creditors *use* financial statements to analyze profitability, liquidity, and solvency.

CHAPTER 3

Accrual and Deferral Timing Differences

The measurement of net income requires that revenue be reported as it is *earned,* and that expenses offset revenue as *incurred,* regardless of when *cash* is received or disbursed. Dividing the life of an enterprise into arbitrary reporting periods—such as quarters or years—makes income measurement challenging, given that many revenue and expense transactions span multiple reporting periods. Thus, it is common for revenue and expenses to occur prior to, or following, the collection or payment of cash. These *timing differences* give rise to revenue and expense *deferrals* and *accruals.*

When *cash collections* occur *before* earning revenue, or *cash disbursements* occur *before* incurring expenses, the cash flow effects on net income must be *deferred* (postponed). Conversely, when *revenue* is earned *before* collecting cash, or expenses are incurred *before* disbursing cash, the income statement effects must be *accrued immediately,* even though related cash flows will not occur until a future reporting period.

Timing Differences

Figure 3.1 summarizes the effects of four common *timing differences* involving cash flows and income measurement:

- *Cash collections* in *prior* periods affect *revenue earned* in the *current* period.
- *Cash payments* in *prior* periods affect *expenses incurred* in the *current* period.

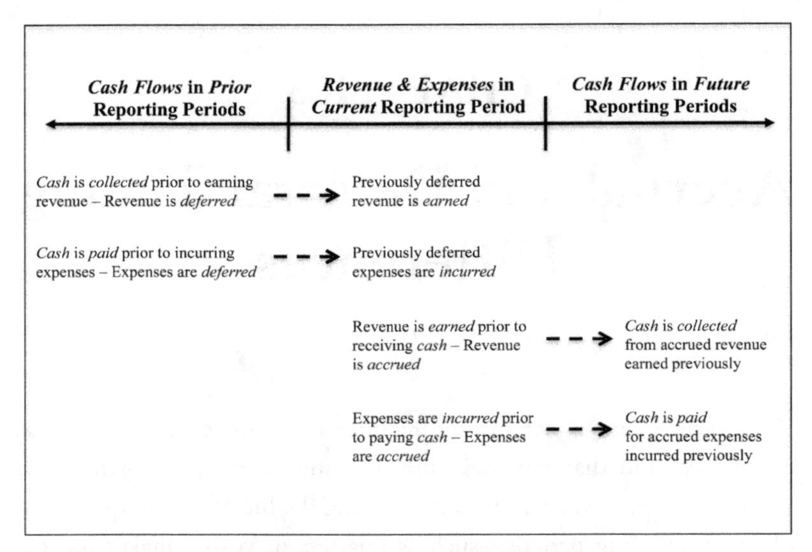

Figure 3.1 Deferral and accrual timing differences

- *Revenues earned* in the *current* period affect *cash collections* in *future* periods.
- *Expenses incurred* in the *current* period affect *cash payments* in *future* periods.

In the first and second timing differences, revenue and expenses were *deferred* (postponed) in a *prior period,* even though cash had been collected or paid. In the third and the fourth timing differences, revenue and expenses are *accrued* and reported immediately in the *current period,* even though cash will not be collected or paid until future periods. Each of these timing differences is discussed separately in the following sections.

Deferred Revenue Timing Differences

Deferred revenue timing differences occur when *cash is received* from customers prior to *revenue being earned.* Revenue was defined in Chapter 2 as increases in assets that result from providing goods and services to customers. In most situations, revenue should be recognized and reported in the income statement whenever all of the following conditions have been met:

- A contract has been established between the seller and the customer.
- The seller's obligation is clearly identified.
- The contract price is measurable.
- The seller's obligation has been satisfied, thereby completing the earnings process.

If one or more of these criteria is not satisfied, the recognition of revenue must be *deferred.*

In many industries, it is common for companies to receive cash from customers before completing the earnings process. For instance, airlines and cruise companies sell tickets well in advance of providing travel services; concert halls sell season tickets prior to performances being given; newspapers sell annual subscriptions before delivering papers; and health spas sell memberships in advance of patrons using their facilities.

Assume that an airline had received $50 million from advance ticket sales in a *prior period.* At the time these bookings were made, contracts had been established, the airline's obligation was clearly identified, and contract prices were measurable. Nevertheless, the *earnings process* was not complete because travelers had not received any flight services.

Thus, the airline *deferred* reporting these advance sales as revenue in the prior period. Instead, it reported a $50 million *liability* in its balance sheet signifying a *future obligation* to either provide flight services or return the money. This obligation appears in the balance sheet as a *current liability* called *unearned ticket revenue.*[1] As flight services for prior period bookings are provided in the *current period,* the $50 million liability in the balance sheet *converts to revenue* reported in the airline's income statement.

Figure 3.2 illustrates the financial statement effects of a deferred revenue timing difference over multiple periods. Notice that as revenue is earned in the current period, the liability—*unearned revenue*—converts into *earned revenue.* The revenue increases net income reported in the income statement, which in turn increases *retained earnings* reported in

[1]A health spa might refer to this liability as unearned membership dues, whereas a newspaper might refer to it as unearned subscription revenue. Regardless of what the obligation is called, it represents a *timing difference* resulting from a *deferral of revenue.*

***Cash* was *received* from customers in a *prior* period, but no revenue was *earned* . . .**

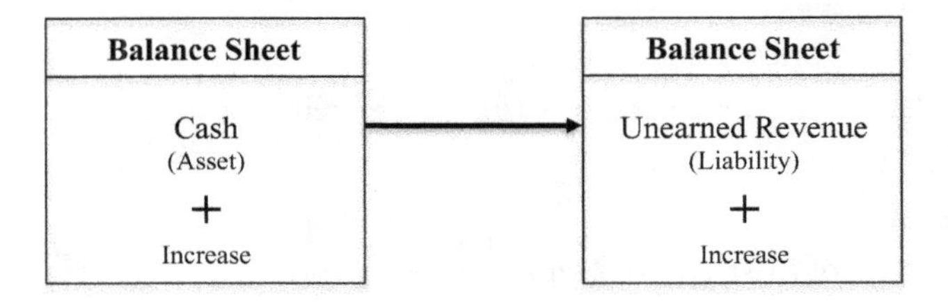

When earned in the *current period, unearned revenue* converts to earned *revenue* . . .

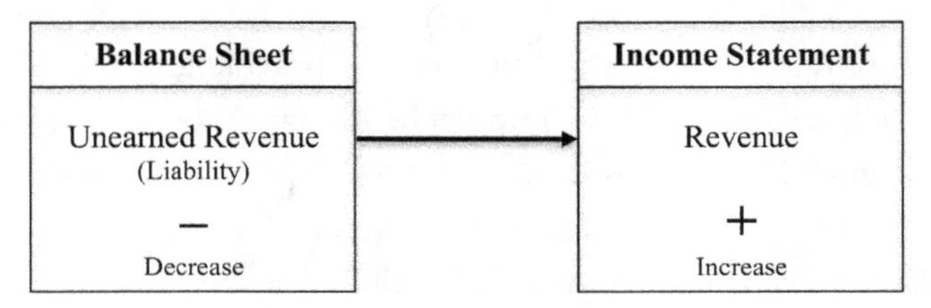

Figure 3.2 Deferred revenue

the shareholders' equity section of the balance sheet. Thus, what was a *liability claim* to assets in the *prior period* is converted to an *equity claim* in the *current period* as revenue is earned.

Deferred Expense Timing Differences

Deferred expense timing differences occur when *cash is paid* prior to *expenses being incurred.* Expenses were defined in Chapter 2 as decreases in assets that result from consuming resources to generate revenue. Until certain assets lose their potential to generate revenue, expenses associated with their acquisition costs are deferred.

As their revenue-generating potential expires over time, these assets convert to expenses, and their costs are *matched* with revenue in the measurement of net income.

Three common activities give rise to deferred expense timing differences: (1) prepaying expenses; (2) acquiring inventory; and (3) investing in fixed assets, such as buildings and equipment.

Prepaid Expense Deferrals

It is not uncommon for companies to pay for certain expenses before matching their costs with revenue in the income statement. For instance, television advertising is usually purchased prior to ads being aired; insurance is purchased prior to a policy's start date; and rent is often paid at the beginning of a rental contract.

Assume that a company paid $12,000 in a *prior period* for a dozen television ads to be aired in a *future period.* Thus, the company initially *deferred* reporting any of this payment as advertising expense. Instead, the entire amount was reported in the balance sheet as a *current asset* with the potential to help generate future revenue. As the ads are aired in the *current period,* the asset—prepaid advertising—*converts to advertising expense* in the company's income statement.

Figure 3.3 illustrates the financial statement effects of timing differences from prepaid expense deferrals over multiple periods. As expenses are incurred in the current period, an asset—*prepaid expenses*—converts into *various expenses.* The expenses decrease net income, which in turn

Cash* was *paid* in a *prior* period, but *no expenses* were *incurred . . .

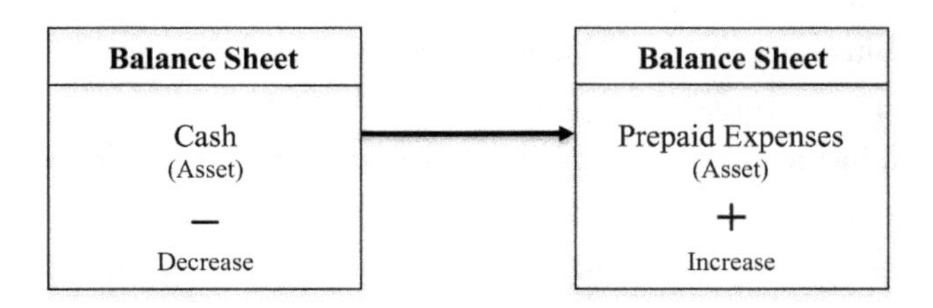

When incurred in the *current period, prepaid expenses* convert to *various expenses . . .*

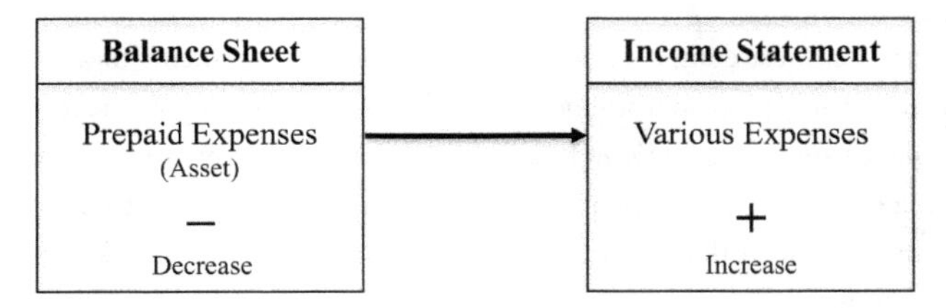

Figure 3.3 Prepaid expense deferrals

decreases *retained earnings* reported in the shareholders' equity section of the balance sheet. Thus, as prepaid expenses provide benefit in the current period, *equity claims* to assets decrease as various expenses are *matched* with revenue.[2]

Inventory Acquisition Deferrals

When companies acquire inventory, they do not immediately deduct its cost from sales revenue reported in the income statement. Instead, the inventory is reported as a resource—a *current asset*—in the balance sheet.[3] Much like the prepaid expenses discussed previously, the income statement effect of acquiring inventory is *deferred* until it can be *matched* with revenue.

Assume that a company purchased inventory in a *prior period* for $5 million, and that none of it was initially sold. Thus, the company *deferred* reporting the cost of this inventory in its prior period income statement. Instead, it reported the inventory in its balance sheet as a current asset with the potential to help generate future revenue. As the inventory is sold in the *current period,* the $5 million asset *converts to cost of goods sold* and is subtracted from sales revenue reported in the income statement.

Figure 3.4 illustrates the financial statement effects of timing differences from inventory acquisition deferrals over multiple periods. As merchandise is sold in the current period, *inventory* converts to *cost of goods sold.* Cost of goods sold decreases net income, which in turn decreases *retained earnings* reported in the shareholders' equity section of the balance sheet. Thus, as merchandise is sold in the current period, *equity claims* to assets decrease as cost of goods sold is *matched* with sales revenue.

---

[2]For reporting purposes, most companies combine all of their prepayments together (such as prepaid advertising, prepaid insurance, and prepaid rent), and report the total amount in the balance sheet as *prepaid expenses.* As these assets convert to expenses (such as advertising expense, insurance expense, and rent expense), these expenses are often combined and appear in the income statement as part of selling, general, and administrative expenses.

[3]Inventory is initially reported as an asset regardless of whether it is purchased in ready-to-sell condition or manufactured, in-house.

***Cash* was *paid* for *inventory* in a *prior* period, but none was *sold* . . .**

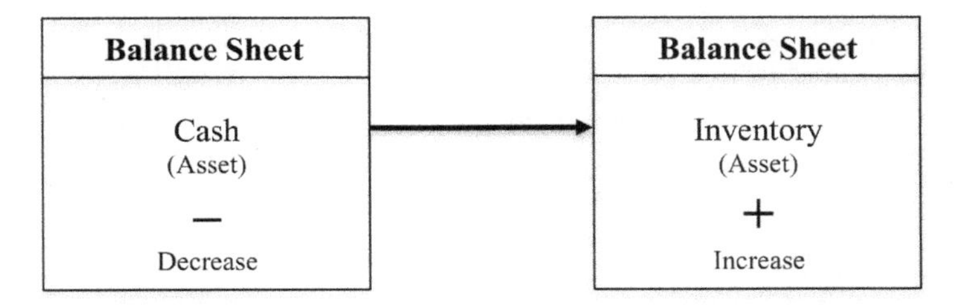

When sold in the *current period, inventory* converts to *cost of goods sold* . . .

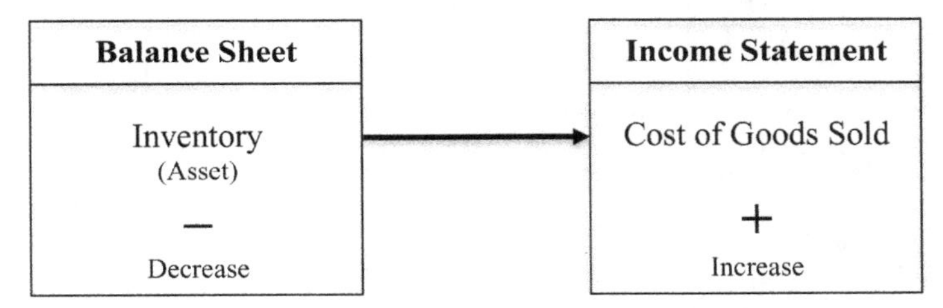

Figure 3.4 Inventory acquisition deferrals

Fixed Asset Investment Deferrals

When companies make investments in fixed assets—such as buildings and equipment—they do not immediately report the cost of these assets in the income statement as deductions from revenue. Instead, they report these investments in the balance sheet as noncurrent assets.[4] As discussed in Chapter 2, the income statement effects of fixed asset acquisitions are initially *deferred,* and subsequently *matched* with revenue over their estimated useful lives.

Assume that in a *prior period* a company acquired equipment costing $4 million. At the time of the purchase, the equipment's estimated useful life was 20 years. Thus, the company initially *deferred* reporting any of the $4 million cost in its income statement. Instead, the entire amount was reported in the balance sheet as a noncurrent *asset.* Each year, as the equipment is used to help generate revenue, $200,000 of its cost in the

[4]Intangible assets—such as patents, copyrights, and trademarks—are accounted for in similar fashion.

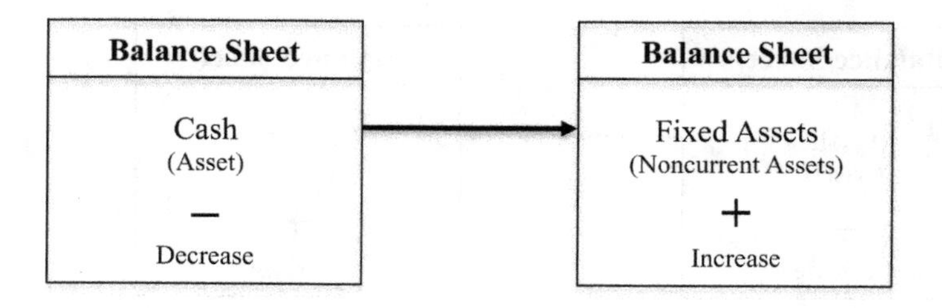

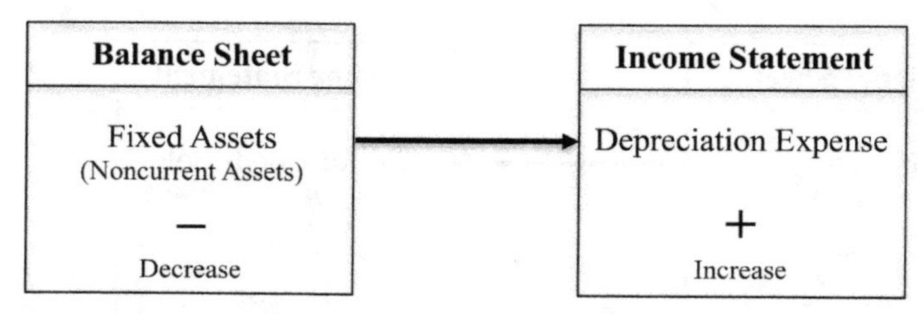

Figure 3.5 Fixed asset investment deferrals

balance sheet converts to depreciation expense in the income statement ($4 million ÷ 20 years = $200,000 per year).

Figure 3.5 illustrates the financial statement effects of timing differences from fixed asset investment deferrals over multiple periods. Each year, a portion of the investment's historical cost converts to *depreciation expense.* Depreciation expense decreases net income reported in the income statement, which in turn decreases *retained earnings* reported in the shareholders' equity section of the balance sheet. Thus, as fixed assets are depreciated in the current period, *equity claims* to assets decrease as depreciation expense is *matched* with revenue.

Accrued Revenue Timing Differences

Accrued revenue timing differences occur when *revenue is earned* prior to *cash being collected.* When credit sales are made to customers, revenue is accrued and reported in the income statement, and an account receivable is reported in the balance sheet. As discussed in Chapter 2, revenue from credit sales is considered *earned* when a contract has been established between a seller and a customer, the seller's obligation is clearly identified, the price is measurable, the seller's obligation has been satisfied, and cash has been received or the likelihood of receiving cash is high.[5]

Many companies make *all* of their sales on credit. For instance, credit sales are commonplace for most wholesalers and manufacturers. These companies often ship large orders to customers worldwide, so collecting cash as deliveries are made is not feasible. In fact, cash sales *exceed* credit sales in only a few industries—examples include retail establishments such as restaurants, grocery stores, and gas stations.[6]

Assume that a company makes credit sales of $10 million in the *current period,* and that no cash will be collected until the *following period.* Thus, revenue of $10 million is reported in its current period income statement, and an account receivable of the same amount is reported in its balance sheet. As collections are made in the *following period,* cash replaces the $10 million accounts receivable in the balance sheet.

Figure 3.6 illustrates the financial statement effects of accrued revenue timing differences over multiple periods. As revenue is *earned* and *accrued* in the current period, accounts receivable—an asset—increases in the balance sheet. The accrued revenue increases net income in the income statement, which in turn increases *retained earnings* in the shareholders' equity section of the balance sheet. Thus, as revenue is accrued, equity claims to assets increase. As collections are received in a *future period,* cash simply replaces accounts receivable in the balance sheet.

Accrued Expense Timing Differences

Accrued expense timing differences occur when *expenses are incurred* prior to *cash being paid.* As unpaid expenses are accrued, they are *matched* with revenue in the income statement, and a liability for the unpaid amount

[5]Not all accrued revenue results from credit sales to customers. Revenue can also accrue on certain fixed-income investments. For instance, *interest revenue* can be earned before receiving any interest payments.

[6]Most retail businesses accept credit cards such as VISA and Discover; however, credit card sales are considered *cash sales* because they provide immediate payments to merchants.

***Revenue* is *earned* in the *current* period, but *no cash* is *collected* . . .**

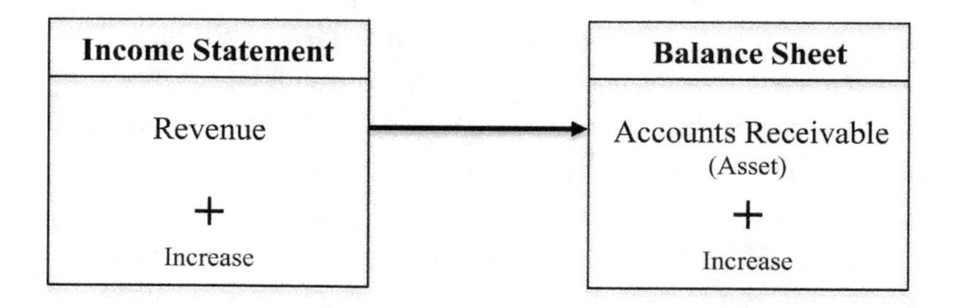

***Accounts receivable* convert to *cash* in a *future* period . . .**

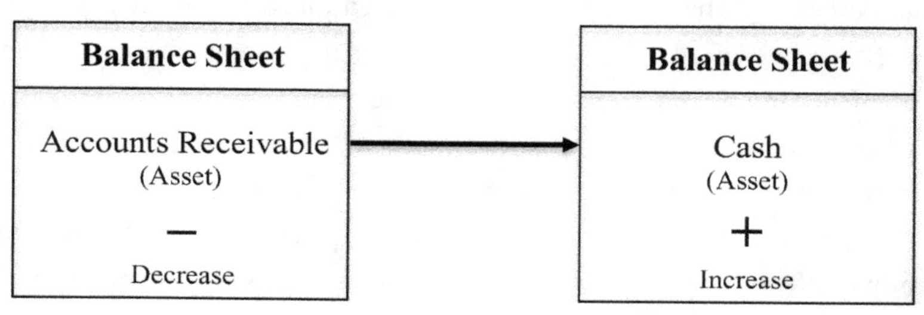

Figure 3.6 Accrued revenue

owed is reported in the balance sheet. There are many situations that give rise to accrued expenses. Three of the most common are accrued payroll expenses, accrued interest expense, and accrued income tax expenses.

Assume that a company processes payroll checks in the *middle* of each month. If its fiscal year ends on December 31, its last payroll distribution for the year will be on or around December 15. Thus, on December 31, it will owe its employees for approximately *two weeks* of work that will not be paid until mid-January of the upcoming year. If on December 31 employees have earned $2 million since being paid on December 15, the company will *accrue* payroll expenses of $2 million to be included in the current year's income statement and report a *current liability*—accrued salaries and wages payable—in the balance sheet for the same amount.

Figure 3.7 illustrates the financial statement effects of accrued expense timing differences over multiple periods. As various expenses are *incurred* and *accrued* in the current period, various payables—liabilities—increase in the balance sheet. The accrued expenses decrease net income in the

***Expenses* are *incurred* in the *current* period, but *no cash* is *paid* . . .**

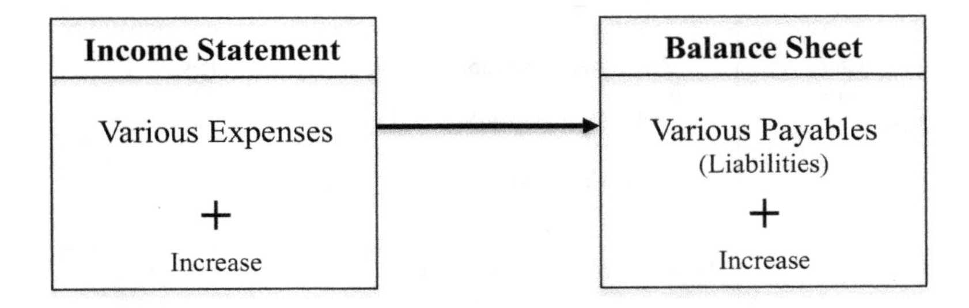

***Various Payables* are settled in a *future* period as *cash* is *paid* . . .**

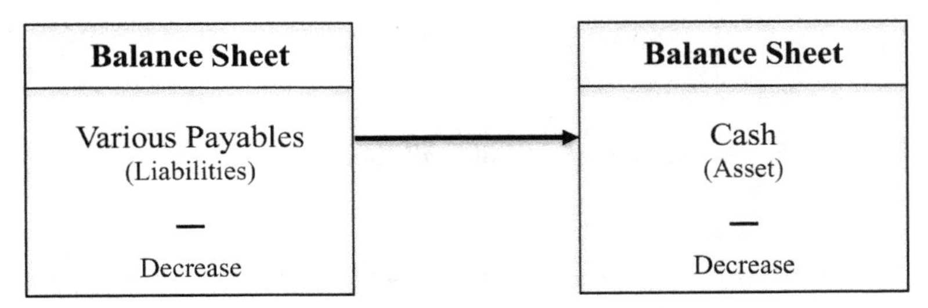

Figure 3.7 Accrued expenses

income statement, which in turn decreases *retained earnings* in the shareholders' equity section of the balance sheet. Thus, as expenses are accrued, equity claims to assets decrease. As payments are made in a *future period,* various accounts payable and cash decrease in the balance sheet.

Summary

If revenue were defined as cash inflow, and expenses were defined as cash outflow, the income statement and the statement of cash flows would be very similar. Such is not the case.

For financial reporting purposes, the income statement reports revenue when it is earned and expenses when they are incurred regardless of when cash is received or paid. Thus, timing differences exist between the components of net income reported in the income statement, and the components of net cash flow reported in the statement of cash flows. The balance sheet *holds* these timing differences until they *reverse.*

	Assets	Liabilities
	Future Cash *Collections*	**Future Cash *Payments***
***Accrual* Timing Differences**	Accounts Receivable Interest Receivable Other Receivables	Salaries Payable Interest Payable Other Payables
	Future *Decreases in Net Income*	**Future *Increases in Net Income***
***Deferral* Timing Differences**	Inventory Prepaid Expenses Depreciable Fixed Assets	Unearned Revenue Unearned Deposits Other Unearned Revenue

Figure 3.8 The balance sheet holds all timing differences

Most assets in the balance sheet are either previously accrued revenue that will increase future cash flow, or previously deferred expenses that will decrease future net income. Likewise, most liabilities reported in the balance sheet are either previously accrued expenses that will decrease future cash flow, or previously deferred revenue that will increase future net income.

Figure 3.8 illustrates how assets and liabilities in the balance sheet *hold* accrual and deferral timing differences examined throughout this chapter. Accrual timing differences reported as assets include various receivables that will become future cash collections, whereas the accrual timing differences held as liabilities include various payables that will become future cash disbursements. Deferral timing differences reported as assets include inventory, prepaid expenses, and depreciable fixed assets that will decrease future net income, whereas the deferral timing differences reported as liabilities include various unearned revenues that will become future increases in net income.

Timing differences play a key role in the coverage of financial statement analysis in Chapter 4. An understanding of deferrals and accruals makes it easy to see how profitable companies can sometimes experience cash flow problems, or how companies with healthy cash flows can sometimes be unprofitable.

CHAPTER 4

Financial Statement Analysis

This chapter is devoted to how external investors and creditors *analyze* financial statements when making resource allocation decisions, specifically, how they use percentages, ratios, and other financial metrics to assess a company's profitability, solvency, and liquidity. Financial statement analysis is complex, and most professional analysts are well versed in accounting, finance, economics, and mathematical modeling. The purpose of this chapter is to provide a *hands-on* introduction of the terminology and concepts unique to this fascinating topic.

The financial statements of a hypothetical retail clothing business—*Fashions By Soges*—will be used to illustrate the analysis process. The discussion will focus on *a single year only*, so trend analysis and financial forecasting will not be addressed. Moreover, there are no *footnotes* accompanying these statements—which for large publicly owned corporations often exceed 100 pages.[1]

Finally, the dollar amounts in Soges' financial statements have been kept purposely small for illustrative purposes. As discussed in Chapter 2, most publicly traded corporations restate their financial reports in thousands or millions of dollars to facilitate analysis. It is important to realize that *absolute* dollar amounts reported in financial statements are less important than the *ratios and proportions* of these figures among one another.

---

[1]Footnotes that accompany actual financial statements are essential to performing financial analysis at an advanced level. Much of the information they convey is highly technical and well beyond the scope of this book.

The Case of Fashions by Soges

At the end of the current year, Soges prepared the four external financial statements discussed in Chapter 2 (the balance sheet, income statement, statement of retained earnings, and statement of cash flows). These statements provide the inputs for analyzing the company's profitability, solvency, and liquidity.

Soges' balance sheet is illustrated in Figure 4.1. Notice that the company's assets grew from $850,000 at the beginning of the year, to $1,349,000 at the end of the year. Equity claims to assets also grew, increasing from $575,000 at the beginning of the year, to $900,000 at the end of the year.

Assets		**December 31**		**January 1**
Current Assets				
Cash	$	59,000	$	50,000
Accounts Receivable (Net)		500,000		100,000
Inventory		115,000		75,000
Other Current Assets		35,000		25,000
Total Current Assets	$	709,000	$	250,000
Noncurrent Assets				
Buildings & Fixtures (Net)	$	440,000	$	400,000
Land		200,000		200,000
Total Noncurrent Assets	$	640,000	$	600,000
Total Assets	$	1,349,000	$	850,000
Liabilities				
Current Liabilities				
Accounts Payable (Trade)	$	185,000	$	85,000
Other Current Liabilities		39,000		40,000
Total Current Liabilities	$	224,000	$	125,000
Noncurrent Liabilities				
Notes Payable	$	225,000	$	150,000
Total Liabilities	$	449,000	$	275,000
Shareholders' Equity				
Common Stock	$	300,000	$	125,000
Retained Earnings		600,000		450,000
Total Shareholders' Equity	$	900,000	$	575,000
Total Liabilities & Shareholders' Equity	$	1,349,000	$	850,000

Figure 4.1 Current year balance sheets

In earlier chapters, the balance sheet was described as a *snapshot* of a company's financial position at a point in time. So ascertaining whether a company is on sound financial footing by looking at the beginning and ending snapshots of its financial position is like attempting to critique a movie by observing only the first and last *frames* of the film. Such would be an exercise in futility.

Although Soges' total assets grew by nearly *60* percent during the year and its shareholders' equity grew by nearly *57* percent, the information conveyed by these two balance sheets provides very little context or meaning. The other three statements are needed to tie them together—much like the middle frames of a movie are needed to convey a story that connects its first frame with its last.

Soges' income statement is illustrated in Figure 4.2. It is clear that the company was profitable, given its reported net income of $156,000 from $900,000 in sales. However, without further analysis, there is no way of assessing the *quality* of these earnings or determining whether net income of $156,000 is adequate.

Notice that *earnings per share* (EPS) of *$1.50* is reported at the bottom of the income statement. EPS was computed by dividing Soges' net income of $156,000 by the 104,000 shares of common stock currently owned by shareholders.

EPS is used to compute a stock's *price–earnings ratio* (PE ratio). PE ratios are computed by dividing a stock's market price by its EPS. Investors

For the Current Year Ending		**December 31**
Net Sales	$	900,000
Cost of Goods Sold		360,000
Gross Profit	$	540,000
Depreciation Expense		20,000
Other Selling, General, & Administrative Expenses		248,000
Operating Income	$	272,000
Interest Expense		12,000
Income Before Income Taxes	$	260,000
Income Taxes		104,000
Net Income	$	156,000
Earnings per Share (104,000 common shares outstanding)	$	1.50

Figure 4.2 Current year income statement

For the Current Year Ending		**December 31**
Beginning Retained Earnings, January 1	$	450,000
Add: Net Income		156,000
Less: Dividends		(6,000)
Ending Retained Earnings, December 31	$	600,000

Figure 4.3 Current statement of retained earnings

and analysts track PE ratios closely to determine whether stock prices are overvalued or undervalued. For instance, if Soges' common stock is currently valued at $15 per share, its PE ratio is *10-to-1* ($15 per share divided by EPS of $1.50). If PE ratios for similar clothing businesses average *6-to-1*, Soges' unusually high PE ratio could be an indication that its stock is overvalued. However, it also could be a signal that investors expect Soges' earnings to increase in the near future.[2]

Soges' statement of retained earnings is shown in Figure 4.3. It reveals that retained earnings grew from $450,000 at the beginning of the year, to $600,000 at the end of the year. It also conveys that $6,000 of the company's net income was distributed in dividends to shareholders during the year. However, without additional information, it is impossible for investors to determine whether a $6,000 dividend is sufficient.

Soges' statement of cash flows is illustrated in Figure 4.4. It provides a detailed reconciliation as to how the company's cash balance grew from $50,000 at the beginning of the year, to $59,000 by the end of the year—an 18 percent increase.

At first glance, Soges' financial statements appear promising. The balance sheet reveals that both assets shareholders' equity grew significantly, the income statement reports that the company was profitable, the statement of retained earnings shows that Soges paid dividends to its shareholders, and the statement of cash flows confirms that the company's cash

[2]Likewise, if stocks of similar clothing companies have PE ratios averaging 15-to-1 (i.e., their stocks are selling at *15 times earnings*), it could be that Soges' stock is undervalued. However, it could also be signal that investors expect Soges' earnings to decrease in the near future. Determining PE ratios for small privately held corporations (like Soges) is challenging because the per share *market values* of their stocks are not readily available.

For the Current Year Ending	**December 31**		
Cash Flow from Operating Activities			
Cash Collected from Customers	$ 500,000		
Cash Paid for Inventory	(300,000)		
Cash Paid for Selling, General, & Administrative Expenses	(363,000)		
Cash Paid for Interest on Long-Term Note Payable	(12,000)		
Net Cash Flow from Operating Activities		$	(175,000)
Cash Flow from Investing Activities			
Cash Paid for the Purchase of Equipment	$ (60,000)		
Net Cash Flow from Investing Activities		$	(60,000)
Cash Flow from Financing Activities			
Net Proceeds from Long-Term Borrowing	$ 75,000		
Net Proceeds from the Issuance of Common Stock	175,000		
Cash Paid for Dividends	(6,000)		
Net Cash Flow from Financing Activities		$	244,000
Net Cash Flow from All Sources		$	9,000
Add: Beginning Cash, January 1			50,000
Ending Cash Reported in Balance Sheet, December 31		$	59,000

Figure 4.4 Current year statement of cash flows

balance increased measurably. Nevertheless, these casual observations certainly do *not* constitute a meaningful analysis. Throughout the remainder of this chapter Soges' financial statements will be used to illustrate a more rigorous assessment of its profitability, solvency, and liquidity.

Profitability

Revenues are increases in assets that result from providing goods and services to customers for a profit, whereas expenses are decreases in assets that result from consuming resources to generate revenue. Thus, when analyzing a company's profitability, it is important to measure how *efficiently* it consumed resources to generate revenue and to increase equity claims to assets. Soges' income statement in Figure 4.2 reports net income of $156,000. The company was definitely profitable, but how efficiently did it consume resources throughout the year to achieve this outcome?

In addressing this question think of two cars, each of which was driven 18,000 miles in the current year. To say that both cars were *effective* at traveling the same distance says nothing about how *efficient* each car was in doing so. For instance, if the first car averaged 36 mpg, it would have consumed 500 gallons of fuel during the year. If the second car averaged 12 mpg, it would have consumed 1,500 gallons of fuel—making it *300 percent less efficient* than the first car in traveling the same distance. So, when evaluating a company's profitability, it is important to focus beyond the bottom line—*the distance traveled*—by taking into account the resources it consumed, its relative size, and the amount of equity capital provided by its shareholders. Four of the most commonly used measures to evaluate a corporation's profitability are its:

- Gross profit percentage;
- Net income percentage;
- Return on equity;
- Return on assets.

Gross Profit Percentage

The gross profit percentage expresses gross profit as a percentage of net sales. In Figure 4.5, Soges' gross profit percentage is computed as *60 percent*. This implies that after deducting the cost of goods sold from net sales, 60 cents of every sales dollar is available to cover the remaining expenses that the company incurred during the year.

To determine whether Soges' gross profit percentage is good or bad, a benchmark of comparison is helpful to see how the company performed relative to other retail clothing businesses of similar size.[3] The industry

Gross Profit (Margin) ÷ Sales

$540,000 ÷ $900,000 = ***60%***

Industry Average = 40%

Figure 4.5 Gross profit percentage

[3]Current industry data are readily available. For instance, Dun & Bradstreet, Inc. prepares *Key Business Ratios* annually for more than 800 types of businesses, and Robert Morris Associates publishes *Annual Statement Studies* from a database of several thousand companies grouped into hundreds of industry classifications and sorted by size.

average for similar retail clothing businesses—those with annual sales and total assets similar in amount to Soges—is only *40 percent.* Thus, it appears that Soges' gross profit percentage is relatively strong.

Net Income Percentage

The net income percentage expresses net income as a percentage of net sales. In Figure 4.6, Soges' net income percentage is computed as *17.3 percent.*

Thus, after deducting the cost of goods sold from net sales, and after covering all of the other costs that the company incurred during the year, approximately 17 cents of every sales dollar is available to retain and reinvest in new assets, or to distribute as dividends to shareholders. The benchmark industry average for this statistic is *4 percent,* so it appears that Soges was extraordinarily efficient at consuming resources to generate revenue.

Return on Equity

Thus far, only Soges' income statement has been used to assess its profitability. Using data from *both* the income statement and the balance sheet provides an expanded perspective of a company's profitability.

Return on equity expresses net income as a percentage of average shareholders' equity reported in the balance sheet. In Figure 4.7, Soges' return on equity is computed as *21.2 percent.* This means that for every dollar of assets financed by shareholders, management was able to generate slightly more than 21 cents in net income. The benchmark industry average is *18 cents,* so it appears that Soges' management team is fairly efficient at converting the shareholder investment into profit.

Net Income ÷ Sales

$156,000 ÷ $900,000 = ***17.3%***

Industry Average = 4%

Figure 4.6 Net income percentage

Net Income ÷ Average Shareholders' Equity

$156,000 ÷ [($575,000 + $900,000)/2] = ***21.2%***

Industry Average = 18%

Figure 4.7 Return on equity

Notice return on equity is computed by dividing net income by a corporation's *average* shareholders' equity. For Soges, average shareholders' equity was computed by adding its beginning shareholders' equity ($575,000) to its ending shareholders' equity ($900,000), and dividing the result by 2. The beginning and ending shareholders' equity figures are snapshots taken at two points in time, whereas net income is a measure of profitability for an entire year. Thus, the argument for using average shareholders' equity in the denominator is to make it more compatible with net income reported in the numerator. Doing so expresses net income earned for the entire year as a percentage of average shareholders' equity for the entire year.

Return on Assets

Return on assets expresses *operating income* as a percentage of average total assets reported in the balance sheet. In Figure 4.8, Soges' return on assets is computed as *24.8 percent.* This statistic measures how efficiently management *squeezed* operating income out of assets under its

Operating Income ÷ Average Total Assets

$272,000 ÷ [(850,000 + $1,349,000)/2] = ***24.8%***

Industry Average = 12%

Figure 4.8 Return on assets

control—regardless of whether assets were financed with debt or with equity. Thus, Soges earned nearly 25 cents in operating income for every dollar of resources at its disposal. The benchmark industry average is only *12 percent*, so at first glance, it appears that assets are being managed efficiently to generate profit.

Notice that *operating income* (income before interest and income taxes) is used in the numerator instead of net income. Given that interest expense and income taxes are determined by factors other than management's ability to manage assets efficiently, they are left out of the computation.[4] The argument for using average total assets in the denominator is the same as using average shareholders' equity to calculate return on equity.

It is important to realize that return on assets does not tell the *whole story* about how efficiently assets have been managed to generate profit. Return on assets should always be broken into its two primary components—*asset turnover* and the *operating income percentage*. Figure 4.9 illustrates these components of return on assets for Soges. Notice that Soges' asset turnover, *multiplied* by its operating income percentage, equals the *return on assets* computed previously in Figure 4.8 (0.819 × 30.2% = *24.8%*).

Asset turnover (sales divided by average total assets) measures how many dollars of sales management generated from the assets it controlled. Soges was able to generate only *81.9 cents* in sales from each asset dollar, whereas the benchmark industry average is *$2* in sales. Thus, it appears that management was not very efficient at using assets to generate sales.

The *operating income percentage* (operating income divided by sales) measures management's efficiency at generating operating income from sales. For every dollar of sales that Soges generated in the current year, it earned *30.2 cents* in operating income. The benchmark industry average is only *6 cents*. Thus, even though Soges generated a relatively low volume of sales from its assets, it was very efficient at converting those sales into operating income.

---

[4]It is not uncommon for some analysts to use *net income* in the numerator rather than *operating income*. Given that interest expense (and its deductibility for tax purposes) is associated with *debt financing* but not *equity financing*, operating income is considered by many to be a better measure of a management's ability control resources, regardless of how those resources were *financed*.

Return on Total Assets = Asset Turnover x Operating Income Percentage

Asset Turnover = Sales ÷ Average Total Assets

$900,000 ÷ [(850,000 + $1,349,000)/ 2] = ***0.819 times***

Operating Income Percentage = Operating Income ÷ Sales

$272,000 ÷ $900,000 = ***30.2%***

Return on Total Assets = 0.819 times x 30.2% = ***24.8%***

Industry Average (Asset Turnover) = 2.0 times

Industry Average (Operating Income Percentage) = 6%

Figure 4.9 Components of return on assets

It is always important to understand industry characteristics when analyzing financial statements. For instance, retail grocery stores and retail jewelry stores both average a return on assets of approximately *12 percent*, albeit for *very different reasons*. Grocery stores have extremely high asset turnovers, but very low operating income percentages. In other words, there is very little profit in a can of beans, so grocery stores must sell *a lot of cans* to survive—as evidenced by their use of a dozen checkout lanes to service multiple customers pushing grocery carts filled with beans. Jewelry stores have extremely low asset turnovers but very high operating income percentages. There is a lot of profit in a gold watch, so jewelry store can survive by selling *relatively few* watches—as evidenced by their use of one or two sales clerks and the absence of customers pushing carts overflowing with gold watches.

In the retail clothing industry, high asset turnover with relatively low operating income percentages is the norm. Oddly, Soges' asset turnover is relatively *low*, and its operating income percentage is unusually *high*. This anomaly would grab the attention of most financial analysts. It will be revisited later in the chapter.

Solvency

Chapter 3 examined *timing differences* that exist between the income statement and the statement of cash flows. Due to timing differences, sales are not a measure of cash inflow, nor are expenses a measure of cash outflow. Accordingly, net income and net cash flow are not interchangeable concepts, and profitability measures are not very useful for assessing solvency or liquidity.

Solvency generally refers to a company's potential to generate enough *cash flow* to satisfy its *long-term* needs, whereas liquidity—discussed in the following section—usually refers to a company's ability to satisfy its *cash flow* obligations in the *immediate future*. Two of the most commonly used measures to evaluate solvency are a company's:

- Debt-to-assets percentage;
- Times interest earned.

Before discussing these measures, it is important to understand that they are directly related to a company's degree of *financial leverage*. Financial leverage refers to a company's reliance upon *debt financing*. Companies that rely heavily on debt financing have *high* degrees of financial leverage, whereas companies that rely very little on debt financing have *low* degrees of financial leverage.[5] High degrees of financial leverage put a company's long-term cash flow potential *at risk*. Indeed, companies buried in debt face a higher risk of defaulting on their legal obligations and being forced into bankruptcy than companies with little or no debt. Thus, solvency issues are of great importance to long-term creditors.

Debt-to-Assets Percentage

The debt-to-assets percentage expresses a company's total liabilities as a percentage of its total assets. A high debt-to-assets percentage is indicative

[5]A company's *degree of financial leverage* can actually be measured and quantified. Doing so is a common practice at more advanced levels of financial analysis than discussed here.

Total Liabilities ÷ Total Assets

$449,000 ÷ $1,349,000 = ***33.3%***

Industry Average = 25%

Figure 4.10 Debt-to-assets percentage

of a high degree of financial leverage, and a greater risk of experiencing solvency problems.[6]

Soges' debt-to-assets percentage is *33.3 percent* at the end of the current year, as shown in Figure 4.10. This means that one-third of its assets are financed with debt, and two-thirds are financed with equity, which is somewhat higher than the benchmark industry average of *25 percent.*

Soges' long-term obligations could relate to the financing of its land and building. Many independent clothing retailers *rent* floor space, which could explain Soges' higher-than-average reliance on debt financing. Useful information pertaining to corporation's long-term obligations is disclosed in the footnotes that accompany the financial statements of actual companies.

Times Interest Earned

Times interest earned—sometimes referred to as the interest coverage ratio—measures *earnings before interest, taxes, depreciation, and amortization* (EBITDA) as a multiple interest expense.[7] In Figure 4.11, Soges' EBITDA is *24 times* its current interest expense, which is *800 percent* more than the benchmark industry average of *3 times*. Thus, even though Soges' 33.3 percent debt-to-assets percentage is somewhat higher than

[6]Many analysts also examine the debt-to-equity percentage when assessing a company's solvency.

[7]EBITDA is computed by *adding* depreciation and amortization expenses to earnings before interest and taxes (EBIT). These expenses are *added* to EBIT because they do *not* require any *future cash payments*. Soges incurred no amortization expense, so only the $20,000 depreciation expense is added to its $272,000 EBIT—its *operating income*—reported in the Figure 4.2 income statement.

EBITDA ÷ Interest Expense

$292,000 ÷ $12,000 = ***24 times***

Industry Average = 3 times

Figure 4.11 Times interest earned

average, the corporation's ability to generate $292,000 of EBITDA to cover its $12,000 interest expense appears outstanding, even if EBITDA decreases significantly in the future.

Liquidity

Liquidity generally refers to a company's ability to satisfy its cash flow obligations in the *immediate future*. Thus, liquidity concerns are of particular interest to short-term creditors. Given the short-term time horizon associated with liquidity, measures to assess it focus on a company's current assets and current liabilities.

Current assets were described in Chapter 2 as resources that provide continuous sources of cash flow to satisfy recurring obligations incurred in daily operations—such as acquiring inventory, paying utility bills, buying insurance, compensating employees, paying taxes, and servicing short-term debts. Most current assets convert into cash in one year or less. *Current liabilities* were described in Chapter 2 as obligations requiring settlement in the same time period that current assets covert into cash.

To remain a sustainable going concern, a company's current assets must consistently generate enough cash to settle its current liabilities. Five of the most commonly used measures to evaluate liquidity are a company's:

- Current ratio;
- Quick ratio;
- Accounts receivable turnover and days;
- Inventory turnover and days;
- Trade payable turnover and days.

Current Assets ÷ Current Liabilities

\$709,000 ÷ \$224,000 = ***3.2-to-1***

Industry Average = 1.4-to-1

Figure 4.12 Current ratio

Current Ratio

The current ratio is computed by dividing a company's *current assets* by its *current liabilities*. Soges' current ratio of *3.2-to-1* at the end of the year is computed in Figure 4.12. Given that current assets are intended to provide a continuous source of cash flow used to satisfy recurring obligations incurred in daily operations, Soges' current assets have the *potential* to generate *\$3.20* for every dollar of current liabilities due in the near future. The benchmark industry average is only *1.4-to-1*.

Quick Ratio

Not all current assets are equally liquid. Inventory, for example, is often replaced by an account receivable when sold—not cash—and prepaid expenses provide a future cash savings, but they do not convert directly into cash. The quick ratio is a more *conservative* measure of liquidity than the current ratio. It is computed by dividing only a company's most liquid current assets by its current liabilities. The assets considered most liquid—often referred to collectively as *financial assets*—include cash, certain marketable securities, and accounts receivable *net* of management's estimate uncollectible accounts.[8]

Soges' quick ratio of *2.5-to-1* is computed in Figure 4.13. The \$559,000 financial assets figure in the numerator is the sum of the

[8]Included with cash reported in the balance sheet are certain *cash equivalents*, such as money market accounts, certificates of deposit, and short-term U.S. Treasury Bills. Marketable securities are *not* considered cash equivalents; moreover, not all marketable securities are included in the computation of the quick ratio. Reporting accounts receivable in the balance sheet *net* of management's estimate of uncollectible accounts was discussed in Chapter 2.

Financial Assets ÷ Current Liabilities
\$559,000 ÷ \$224,000 = ***2.5-to-1***
Industry Average = 0.6-to-1

Figure 4.13 Quick ratio

company's cash (\$59,000) and its net accounts receivable (\$500,000) at the end of the year. Soges' financial assets have the *potential* to generate *\$2.50* for every dollar of current liabilities due in the near future. The benchmark industry average is only *0.60-to-1*.

Two of Soges' liquidity measures—the current ratio and the quick ratio—indicate that the company's short-term cash flow position is *very strong*. That said, it is important to bear in mind that both of these ratios were computed using *only* balance sheet information. Thus, these measures are static snapshots of the company's liquidity at the end of the current year. They provide no insight regarding *how quickly* the company's current assets are converting to cash, or how *quickly* the company's current liabilities are being settled. Using data from *both* the income statement and the balance sheet provides information about how efficiently receivables, inventories, and trade payables are being managed.

Accounts Receivable Turnover and Days

Soges' accounts receivable turnover is computed in Figure 4.14 by dividing its sales of \$900,000 by its average accounts receivable of \$300,000.

The resulting computations show that Soges *turned over* its accounts receivable only *3 times* during the entire year—meaning that the company's average receivable balance of \$300,000 was collected and converted to cash just 3 times in 365 days.[9] Dividing 365 days by Soges' turnover

[9]The \$900,000 sales figure was taken from the income statement in Figure 4.2. The average accounts receivable balance of \$300,000 was computed by adding the accounts receivable at the beginning of the year (\$100,000) to accounts receivable at the end of the year (\$500,000), and dividing the result by 2. The accounts receivable amounts were taken from the balance sheet in Figure 4.1.

Accounts Receivable Turnover = Sales ÷ Average Accounts Receivable

$900,000 ÷ [($100,000 + $500,000)/2] = ***3.0 times***

Accounts Receivable Days = 365 Days ÷ Accounts Receivable Turnover

365 Days ÷ 3.0 times = ***122 days***

Industry Average (Accounts Receivable Turnover) = 36 times

Industry Average (Accounts Receivable Days) = 10 days

Figure 4.14 Accounts receivable turnover and days

statistic reveals that its credit accounts remain outstanding an average of *122 days* before being collected.

The benchmark industry average for accounts receivable turnover is *36 times*, whereas the average amount of time that credit accounts remain outstanding is *10 days*. Based on this information, it appears that Soges is doing a *very poor job* of managing its credit accounts.

Inventory Turnover and Days

Soges' inventory turnover is computed in Figure 4.15 by dividing its cost of goods sold of $360,000 by its average inventory balance of $95,000.[10]

The resulting computations show that Soges *turned over* its inventory only *3.8 times* during the entire year—meaning that the company's average inventory of $95,000 was sold and replenished less than 4 times in 365 days. Dividing 365 days by the turnover statistic in Figure 4.15 reveals that Soges' inventory items remain in stock an average of *96 days* before being sold.

The benchmark industry average for inventory turnover is *12 times*, whereas the average amount of time that inventory remains in stock is

[10]The $360,000 cost of goods sold figure was taken from the income statement in Figure 4.2. The average inventory balance of $95,000 was computed by adding inventory on hand at the beginning of the year ($75,000) to inventory on hand at the end of the year ($115,000), and dividing the result by 2. The inventory amounts were taken from the balance sheet in Figure 4.1.

Inventory Turnover = Cost of Goods Sold ÷ Average Inventory

$360,000 ÷ [($75,000 + $115,000)/2] = ***3.8 times***

Inventory Days = 365 Days ÷ Inventory Turnover

365 Days ÷ 3.8 times = ***96 days***

Industry Average (Inventory Turnover) = 12 times

Industry Average (Inventory Days) = 37 days

Figure 4.15 Inventory turnover & days

37 days. Based on this information, it appears that Soges is mismanaging inventory, as well.

Trade Payable Turnover and Days

As discussed in Chapter 2, *trade* accounts payable result from purchasing inventory on credit. Soges' trade payable turnover is computed in Figure 4.16 by dividing its inventory *purchases* of $400,000 by its average trade payable balance of $135,000.[11]

The resulting computations convey that Soges *turned over* its trade payables *2.96 times* during the entire year—meaning that the company's average trade payable balance of $135,000 was settled with cash approximately 3 times in 365 days. Dividing 365 days by the turnover statistic in Figure 4.16 reveals that Soges' trade payables remain outstanding an average of *123 days* before being paid.

[11]Inventory *purchases* of $400,000 were computed by subtracting inventory at the beginning of the year ($75,000) from inventory at the end of the year ($115,000), and adding the result to cost of goods sold ($360,000). The average trade payables balance of $135,000 was computed by adding the company's trade payables at the beginning of the year ($85,000) to its trade payables at the end of the year ($185,000), and dividing the result by 2. The inventory and trade payable figures were taken from the balance sheet in Figure 4.1. The cost of goods sold figure was taken from the income statement in Figure 4.2.

Trade Payable Turnover = Inventory Purchases ÷ Average Trade Payables

$400,000 ÷ [($85,000 + $185,000)/2] = ***2.96 times***

Trade Payable Days = 365 Days ÷ Trade Payable Turnover

365 Days ÷ 2.96 times = ***123 days***

Industry Average (Trade Payable Turnover) = 24 times

Industry Average (Trade Payable Days) = 15 days

Figure 4.16 Trade payable turnover & days

The benchmark industry average for trade payable turnover is *24 times*, whereas the average amount of time that trade payables remains outstanding is *15 days*. Based on this information, it appears that Soges' largest current assets—accounts receivable and inventory—are not providing the continuous cash flow required to satisfy inventory purchases on a timely basis. Indeed, cash is tied up in inventory for *96 days* before being sold, after which it remains tied up in accounts receivable for another *122 days* before being collected.[12] Meanwhile, the company is struggling to settle its trade payables every *123 days*. This situation is *not sustainable*. So what exactly went wrong?

Profit Rich but Cash Poor

The predicament faced by Soges is a classic example of being profit rich but cash poor. Figure 4.17 provides a recap of Soges' profitability, solvency, and liquidity measures.

[12]The cyclical process of recovering cash invested in inventory was described in Chapter 2 as an *operating cycle*. Soges' operating cycle takes *218 days* to complete—96 days to sell the merchandise it has in stock, plus 122 days to collect cash from its customers. The benchmark industry average for similar clothing businesses is *47 days*—37 days to sell inventory, plus 10 days to collect cash from customers.

In terms of *profitability*, the company's performance was stellar. Its gross profit percentage, net income percentage, operating income percentage, and return on assets were outstanding, and its return on equity was on the high-end of normal. *Solvency* measures seem to indicate that Soges' long-term cash flow potential is favorable, with a debt-to-assets percentage in the normal range accompanied by an exceptionally strong interest coverage ratio. Even its current and quick ratios imply that the company should not encounter any liquidity problems satisfying its current obligations as they come due—but these two measures are static snapshots of liquidity taken from the balance sheet.

Problems in Paradise

An examination of Soges' *turnover* measures conveys an entirely different story regarding its liquidity—accounts receivable are not being collected in a timely manner, inventory is not selling fast enough, and payments of trade payables are being delayed well beyond what is acceptable. A hint that these problems existed arose during the analysis of Soges' *profitability*. The company's only *red flag* was its alarmingly weak *asset turnover* statistic

Profitability	**Figure**	**Soges**	**Average**	**Assessment**
Gross Profit Percentage	**4.5**	60.0%	40.0%	Strong
Net Income Percentage	**4.6**	17.3%	4.0%	Strong
Return on Equity	**4.7**	21.2%	18.0%	Normal
Return on Assets	**4.8**	24.8%	12.0%	Strong
Asset Turnover	**4.9**	0.819 times	2 times	Weak
Operating Income Percentage	**4.9**	30.2%	6.0%	Strong
Solvency	**Figure**	**Soges**	**Average**	**Assessment**
Debt-to-Asset Percentage	**4.10**	33.3%	25.0%	Normal
Interest Coverage Ratio	**4.11**	24 times	3 times	Strong
Liquidity	**Figure**	**Soges**	**Average**	**Assessment**
Current Ratio	**4.12**	3.2-to-1	1.4-to-1	Strong
Quick Ratio	**4.13**	2.5-to-1	.06-to-1	Strong
Accounts Receivable Turnover	**4.14**	3 times	36 times	Weak
Accounts Receivable Days	**4.14**	122 days	10 days	Weak
Inventory Turnover	**4.15**	3.8 times	12 times	Weak
Inventory Days	**4.15**	96 days	37 days	Weak
Trade Payable Turnover	**4.16**	2.96 times	24 times	Weak
Trade Payable Days	**4.16**	123 days	15 days	Weak

Figure 4.17 Financial analysis recap

(computed by dividing sales by average total assets)—which means that the company has too much invested in assets given its current level of sales. An important question is whether any *specific assets* have grown too large relative to its sales.

Soges' balance sheet in Figure 4.1 reveals that accounts receivable and inventory comprise *46 percent* of total assets at the *end* of the year—by comparison, they accounted for just *21 percent* of total assets at the *beginning* of the year. Together, these two accounts increased during the year by more than *350 percent*. These two accounts grew because they were not *turning over*. Had the company's accounts receivable and inventory turnover measures been more in line with industry averages, its asset turnover would have been normal, and its liquidity problems would not have existed. Unfortunately, the *timing differences* between Soges' income statement and its statement of cash flows are severe—as evidenced by comparing its operating income of $272,000 into its negative cash flow from operating activities of $175,000.[13]

Liquidity problems resulting from timing differences are not uncommon. They frequently occur when companies experience *rapid growth* accompanied by a surge in their inventories and accounts receivable. As growth levels off, inventory investment stabilizes, accounts receivable are collected, and liquidity problems usually subside.

Summary

This chapter provided a *hands-on* introduction of basic financial analysis techniques used by investors and creditors. It was intended to achieve two goals. The first goal was to demonstrate how financial statement information is used to compute percentages, ratios, and other financial metrics to gain insight pertaining to a company's profitability, solvency, and liquidity. The second goal was to illustrate how *timing differences* between income and cash flow can cause companies to be *profit rich, but cash poor*.[14]

The importance of understanding timing differences is not confined to investors and creditors. In later chapters, timing differences will be revisited from a *managerial perspective* and examined in a budgetary context.

[13]The operating income figure appears in the Figure 4.2 income statement. The negative cash flow from operating activities figure appears in the Figure 4.4 statement of cash flows.

[14]Timing differences also can cause companies to be *profit poor, but cash rich*.

CHAPTER 5

Long-Term Financial Forecasting

Chapter 4 provided an introductory overview of financial statement analysis. The focus of Chapter 4 was *historical*—meaning that financial statements were used to analyze how profitable, solvent, and liquid a company had been in the *past.* The focus of this chapter is forward-looking—meaning that it examines how accounting information is used to forecast a company's potential financial performance in the *future.*

Financial forecasting can cover both short-term time horizons (such as months or quarters) and long-term time horizons that span multiple years. Short-term forecasting (often called *operational budgeting*) is primarily a managerial activity performed by internal users of financial information. Short-term forecasting is illustrated in Chapter 6.

Both internal and external users of financial information engage in long-term forecasting. Throughout this chapter long-term forecasting is examined from a managerial perspective. The material builds upon financial statement integration discussed in Chapter 2, timing differences addressed in Chapter 3, and applications profitability and liquidity measures introduced in Chapter 4.

Long-Term Financial Forecasting: An Overview

The goal of long-term financial forecasting is to create projected financial statements (and other important information) that will enable internal and external decision makers to better assess the timing, the amounts, and the uncertainties associated with an entity's future earnings, its ongoing changes in financial position, and its potential to generate long-term cash flow.

Managers and other internal decision makers rely heavily upon long-term forecasts. Long-term projections are instrumental when planning investing activities, such as those related to fixed asset growth, equipment replacements, and capital leasing arrangements. They enable managers to budget for changes in technology, plan for product line diversification, and orchestrate mergers with—or acquisitions of—other companies. Long-term financial forecasts also assist managers as they grapple with complex workforce decisions, including pension fund structuring, early retirement incentives, downsizing, and the possibility of offshore manufacturing. Moreover, they are used to plan for, and to analyze, a variety of long-term financing decisions, such as the timing of an initial public offering, the issuance of bonds, or the refinancing of a mortgage.

External stakeholders also engage in long-term financial forecasting. Investors are keenly interested in the timing, amounts, and uncertainties about a corporation's future dividend activity. Long-term dividend projections—in conjunction with various other forecasted data—are used to discern whether the current price of a company's stock is realistic and to make informed predictions about its future growth potential. Creditors also engage in long-term financial forecasting to predict anticipated changes in a company's capital structure, assess a borrower's debt servicing potential, analyze probabilities of default, and negotiate troubled debt restructuring arrangements.

Long-term financial forecasts typically do not focus upon detailed operating activities such as accounts receivable collection schedules, raw materials acquisition plans, weekly production level targets, or other issues related to working capital management. These are short-term forecasting concerns that will be addressed in Chapter 6. Long-term financial forecasting has a much broader focus, much of which is related to macroeconomic variables. As such, it requires an understanding of monetary policy and how it relates to inflation and interest rate variability; fiscal policy and how it is tied to possible changes in the tax law legislation and tax rates; and foreign policies that affect global competition, the strength of the U.S. dollar, and the political stability of governments in other countries.

The creation and use of long-term financial forecasts will be illustrated with a short case throughout the remainder of this chapter. The case illustrates how managers of a hardware business use long-term forecasts to address and hopefully quell solvency concerns voiced by its major creditor.

The Case of Hometown Hardware

Hometown Hardware is a closely held corporation owned by McNamer Enterprises (a small group of investors). A loyal team of employees manages the business, and under its leadership, sales have steadily increased over the past several years. Although the company is profitable, its cash flow from operating activities is consistently negative, and it continually struggles with liquidity problems.

The shareholders of McNamer Enterprises believe in Hometown's potential, yet they are frustrated that they have not received dividends for several years. To keep Hometown from depleting all of its cash reserves, McNamer Enterprises recently invested an additional $50,000 in exchange for shares of common stock, with a stipulation that a dividend of $125,000 must be distributed within *2 years*. Even with this liquidity infusion, Hometown's cash balance has fallen during the current year from $24,500 in early January, to $3,000 at the end of the year.

Hometown's balance sheet shows a relatively strong financial position with total assets of $1,500,000 and shareholders' equity claims of $1,000,000. Moreover, its current and quick ratios of 4.93-to-1 and 2.82-to-1 are well above industry averages. The seemingly strong liquidity position reflected in the balance sheet is confusing to management, given the company's cash flow problems.

Hometown extends credit to numerous commercial customers, most of whom are construction contractors. The company's accounts receivable turnover rate of 5 times (72 days) is well below the industry average of 8 times (45 days), and its inventory turnover rate of 4 times (90 days) is significantly below the industry average of 9 times (40 days). Its trade payable turnover rate is 6 times (60 days), compared to an industry average of 12 times (30 days).

Hometown's balance sheet reports a $400,000 long-term note payable owed to a local bank. The annual debt service cost on this note is $48,000, of which $10,000 will be allocated to interest expense for the upcoming year, and $8,000 will be allocated to interest expense the following year.[1]

[1]The annual debt service cost of $48,000 is a *fixed* payment that is allocated between interest expense and the payback of the note's outstanding principal. As the principal of the note declines over time, the amount of the $48,000 that is allocated to interest expense declines, as well.

The company has fallen into a pattern of being late in making its debt service payments. As such, the bank's loan officers are extremely uncomfortable and worry about the company's ability to service the $400,000 obligation. They met with the Hometown's management near the *end* of the *current year* and demanded that they develop a financial plan to resolve the company's cash flow problems. As part of the plan, they requested a complete set of *financial statement forecasts* for the next *2 years* (Year-2 and Year-3). The forecasts are due the first week of the upcoming year (Year-2).

To improve cash flow, Hometown intends to implement tighter credit policies and offer credit customers financial incentives for paying on time. Management is confident that Year-2 accounts receivable turnover can be increased to 6 times (60 days), and that the industry average of 8 times (45 days) will be achieved by the end of Year-3.

The company's computer system is antiquated and frequently crashes. Management believes that investing in a new system costing $120,000 will drastically improve the monitoring of accounts receivable, inventory, and trade payables. To that end, the company will invest in a new system during the first quarter of Year-2. Once operational, management predicts that Year-2 inventory turnover will improve to 5 times (72 days), and that the industry average of 9 times (40 days) will be achieved by the end of Year-3. In addition, management is hopeful that the new system will enable Hometown to increase Year-2 trade payables turnover to 8 times (45 days), and achieve the industry average of 12 times (30 days) by the end of Year-3. The new system is will increase the company's annual depreciation expense by $15,000 in Year-2 and Year-3.

To raise additional cash, management intends to sell a parcel of land to a developer in Year-2. Hometown purchased the land 10 years ago for $40,000 with the intention of using it as a site for a warehouse facility; however, that plan has been abandoned. Unfortunately, due to a depressed real estate market, the developer is willing to pay only $25,000, which will result in a $15,000 loss on the sale.[2]

---

[2]The $15,000 loss on the sale is computed by subtracting the $25,000 selling price from the original purchase price of $40,000.

Management expects sales to increase by 10 percent in Year-2, and increase an additional 12 percent in Year-3. Cost of goods sold as a percentage of sales is expected to remain constant at 60 percent for the next 2 years—meaning gross profit will remain at 40 percent of sales. Selling, general, and administrative (SG&A) expenses are projected to increase by 2 percent in Year-2, and by an additional 3 percent in Year-3. The company's accountant believes that the average income tax rate will hold steady for the next 2 years at 30 percent.

Figure 5.1 provides a summary of the input variables necessary to prepare *2 years* of financial forecasts (Year-2 and Year-3). It also includes *actual data* from its *current year* of operations.

From the input data summarized in Figure 5.1, projected income statements, balance sheets, and statements of cash flows were created for Year-2 and Year-3. The statement of retained earnings is embedded in the shareholders' equity section of each balance sheet.

Input Variables	Current Year Actual	Year-2 Projections	Year-3 Projections
Percentage Increase in Net Sales	-	10%	12%
Cost of Goods Sold - % of Net Sales	60%	60%	60%
Increase in SG & A Expenses	-	2%	3%
Income Tax Rate	30%	30%	30%
Accounts Recivable Turnover (Times per Year)	5	6	8
Inventory Turnover (Times per Year)	4	5	9
Trade Payable Turnover (Times per Year)	6	8	12
Historical Cost of Land Sold	$ -	$ 40,000	$ -
Cash Proceeds from Sale of Land	-	25,000	-
Loss on Sale of Land	$ -	$ 15,000	$ -
Purchase Computer System	$ -	$ 120,000	$ -
Depreciation - Building, Fixtures, & Equipment	$ 40,000	$ 55,000	$ 55,000
Debt Service Cost of Long-Term Note Payable	$ 48,000	$ 48,000	$ 48,000
Interest Portion of Debt Service Payment	15,000	12,000	10,000
Principal Portion of Debt Service Payment	$ 33,000	$ 36,000	$ 38,000
Issued Common Stock	$ 50,000	$ -	$ -
Cash Dividends	$ -	$ -	$ 125,000

***Figure 5.1** Summary of forecasting variables: year-2 and year-3*

Forecasted Income Statements

Long-term financial forecasts begin with the preparation of forecasted income statements. Hometown's actual income statement for the current year and its projected income statements for Year-2 and Year-3 appear in Figure 5.2.

All of the revenue and expense amounts appearing in Figure 5.2 came directly from the input data in Figure 5.1. Projected sales of $1,540,000 in Year-2 represent a 10 percent increase over the current year's actual sales of $1,400,000, whereas sales of $1,724,800 in Year-3 represent a 12 percent increase over Year-2 sales. The cost of goods sold reported in Year-2 and Year-3 is simply 60 percent of each year's anticipated sales.

Projected SG&A expenses of $510,000 in Year-2 represent a 2 percent increase over the current year's actual SG&A expenses of $500,000. The $525,300 SG&A figure in Year-3 represents a 3 percent increase over the SG&A amount in Year-2. All of Hometown's SG&A expenses are paid in cash as they are incurred.

The projected $15,000 loss on the sale land in Year-2 is the land's $40,000 original cost less the anticipated sales proceeds of $25,000. Projected interest expenses of $12,000 in Year-2 and $10,000 in Year-3 reflect the amount of Hometown's annual $48,000 debt service cost allocated to interest in those 2 years. Projected income tax expenses of $7,200 in Year-2 and $29,886 in Year-3 equal 30 percent of each year's projected income before taxes.

INCOME STATEMENT	Current Year Actual	Year-2 Projections	Year-3 Projections
Net Sales	$ 1,400,000	$ 1,540,000	$ 1,724,800
Cost of Goods Sold	840,000	924,000	1,034,880
Gross Profit	$ 560,000	$ 616,000	$ 689,920
Selling, General, & Administrative Expenses	500,000	510,000	525,300
Depreciation Expense	40,000	55,000	55,000
Loss on Sale of Land	-	15,000	-
Income Before Interest & Taxes	$ 20,000	$ 36,000	$ 109,620
Interest Expense	15,000	12,000	10,000
Income Before Taxes	$ 5,000	$ 24,000	$ 99,620
Taxes	1,500	7,200	29,886
Net Income	$ 3,500	$ 16,800	$ 69,734

Figure 5.2 Projected income statements: year-2 and year-3

Forecasted Balance Sheets

Hometown's forecasted balance sheets are presented in Figure 5.3. At first glance, it appears that the company's cash position is expected to improve significantly in Year-2 and Year-3. Before discussing this improvement, it is important to understand how each of the *other* balance sheet items was derived.

Accounts Receivable

Accounts receivable for Year-2 and Year-3 was projected by dividing each year's sales in the Figure 5.2 income statements by the corresponding accounts receivable turnover targets summarized in Figure 5.1:

Sales ÷ Accounts Receivable Turnover = Projected Accounts Receivable

BALANCE SHEET	Current Year Actual	Year-2 Projections	Year-3 Projections
ASSETS			
Cash	$ 3,000	$ 19,683	$ 60,370
Accounts Receivable	280,000	256,667	215,600
Inventory	210,000	184,800	114,987
Total Current Assets	$ 493,000	$ 461,150	$ 390,956
Building, Fixturess & Equipment (Net)	$ 842,000	$ 907,000	$ 852,000
Land	165,000	125,000	125,000
Total Non Current Assets	$ 1,007,000	$ 1,032,000	$ 977,000
Total Assets	$ 1,500,000	$ 1,493,150	$ 1,367,956
LIABILITIES			
Trade Payables	$ 100,000	$ 112,350	$ 80,422
Long-Term Notes Payable	400,000	364,000	326,000
Total Liabilities	$ 500,000	$ 476,350	$ 406,422
SHAREHOLDERS' EQUITY			
Common Stock	$ 800,000	$ 800,000	$ 800,000
Beginning Retained Earnings	$ 196,500	$ 200,000	$ 216,800
Add: Net Income	3,500	16,800	69,734
Less: Dividends	-	-	(125,000)
Ending Retained Earnings	$ 200,000	$ 216,800	$ 161,534
Total Shareholders' Equity	$ 1,000,000	$ 1,016,800	$ 961,534
Total Liabilities & Shareholders' Equity	$ 1,500,000	$ 1,493,150	$ 1,367,956

***Figure 5.3** Projected year-end balance sheets: year-2 and year-3*

Using this approach, the projected accounts receivable amounts reported in the Figure 5.3 balance sheets are:

- *Year-2:* \$1,540,000 ÷ 6 times = \$256,667 projected accounts receivable
- *Year-3:* \$1,724,800 ÷ 8 times = \$215,600 projected accounts receivable.

Inventory

Inventory in Year-2 and Year-3 was projected by dividing each year's cost of goods sold in the Figure 5.2 income statements by the corresponding inventory turnover targets summarized in Figure 5.1:

Cost of Goods Sold ÷ Inventory Turnover = Projected Inventory

Thus, the projected inventory amounts reported in the Figure 5.3 balance sheets are:

- *Year-2:* \$924,000 ÷ 5 times = \$184,800 projected inventory
- *Year-3:* \$1,034,880 ÷ 9 times = \$114,987 projected inventory.

Land

Year-2 and Year-3 land amounts were projected by adjusting each year's beginning figure by anticipated acquisition and sales activities summarized in Figure 5.1:

Beginning Land + Land Purchased – Land Sold = Projected Land

Accordingly, the projected land figures reported in the Figure 5.3 balance sheets are[3]:

- *Year-2:* \$165,000 + \$0 – \$40,000 = \$125,000 projected land
- *Year-3:* \$125,000 + \$0 – \$0 = \$125,000 projected land.

---

[3]Land at the *beginning* of Year-2 is the \$165,000 actual amount reported in the balance sheet at the *end* of the *current year.* Likewise, land at the *beginning* of Year-3 is the \$125,000 projected amount reported at the *end* of Year-2. The \$40,000 *historical cost* of the land that was sold in Year-2 is subtracted from the amount of land at the beginning of Year-2, *not* its \$25,000 *selling price.* No land was purchased in either year.

Depreciable Fixed Assets

Hometown's buildings, fixtures, and equipment (BFE) are the company's *depreciable fixed assets.* As discussed previously, these assets are reported in the balance sheet at historical cost *net* of accumulated depreciation from prior years.[4] The projected BFE amounts in Year-2 and Year-3 were projected by adjusting BFE at the beginning of each year by the events summarized in Figure 5.2 that are anticipated to occur during the year:

Beginning BFE + BFE Purchased – BFE Sold – Depreciation Expense = Projected BFE

Using this approach, the projected BFE amounts reported in the Figure 5.3 balance sheets are[5]:

- *Year-2:* \$842,000 + \$120,000 – \$0 – \$55,000 = \$907,000 projected BFE
- *Year-3:* \$907,000 + \$0 – \$0 – \$55,000 = \$852,000 projected BFE.

Trade Payables

Trade payables are current liabilities owed for inventory purchased on credit. To forecast trade payables, future inventory *purchases* must be determined first.[6] Inventory purchases can be projected as follows:

Cost of Goods Sold + Ending Inventory – Beginning Inventory = Projected Inventory Purchases

---

[4]As explained in Chapter 2, land is *not* considered a depreciable fixed asset because its useful life is unlimited.

[5]BFE at the *beginning* of Year-2 is the \$842,000 actual amount reported in the balance sheet at the *end* of the *current year.* Likewise, BFE at the *beginning* of Year-3 is the \$907,000 projected amount reported at the *end* of Year-2. No BFE sales are anticipated in either year.

[6]Some analysis forecast trade payables based on *cost of goods sold* rather than inventory *purchases.* This practice is not recommended unless inventory amounts are relatively constant from year to year.

Projected cost of goods sold in Year-2 and Year-3 is reported in the Figure 5.2 income statements. The inventory figures for Year-2 and Year-3 are reported in the Figure 5.3 balance sheets. The beginning Year-2 inventory is the actual ending inventory figure reported in the current-year balance sheet. The beginning inventory for Year-3 is the projected ending inventory for Year-2. Thus, projected inventory purchases for Year-2 and Year-3 are computed as follows:

- *Year-2:* $924,000 + $184,800 − $210,000 = $898,800 projected inventory purchases
- *Year-3:* $1,034,880 + $114,987 − $184,800 = $965,067 projected inventory purchases.

Using projected inventory purchases and dividing by the corresponding trade payable turnover targets from Figure 5.1, projected trade payable amounts are computed as follows:

Inventory Purchases ÷ Trade Payables Turnover = Projected Trade Payables

Thus, the trade payable projections reported in the Figure 5.3 balance sheets are:

- *Year-2:* $898,800 ÷ 8 times = $112,350 projected trade payables
- *Year-3:* $965,067 ÷ 12 times = $80,422 projected trade payables.

Long-Term Notes Payable

The long-term notes payable projections in Year-2 and Year-3 were derived in the following manner:

Beginning Notes Payable + New Borrowing – Principal Payments = Projected Notes Payable

Hometown does not anticipate any new borrowing in Year-2 or Year 3, so the only adjustment to the beginning balance each year is the annual principal payment shown in Figure 5.1. Thus, the long-term note payable projections reported in the Year-2 and Year-3 balance sheets are:

- *Year-2:* $400,000 + $0 − $36,000 = $364,000 projected long-term note payable
- *Year-3:* $364,000 + $0 − $38,000 = $326,000 projected long-term note payable.

Common Stock

Common stock at the end of Year-2 and Year-3 was projected by increasing the beginning amounts by the anticipated issuances of new stock to investors each year:

Beginning Common Stock + New Stock Issued = Projected Common Stock

Hometown does not anticipate any new stock issues, so the *actual* amount reported in its current-year balance sheet is carried forward to the Year-2 and Year-3 balance sheets, as follows:

- *Year-2:* $800,000 + $0 = $800,000 projected common stock
- *Year-3:* $800,000 + $0 = $800,000 projected common stock.

Retained Earnings

Changes to retained earnings in Year-2 and Year-3 are embedded in the shareholders' equity section of the Figure 5.3 balance sheets. The projections follow the same format as a statement of retained earnings:

Beginning Retained Earnings + Income − Dividends = Projected Retained Earnings

Thus, the projected retained earnings amounts reported in the Figure 5.3 balance sheets are[7]:

- *Year-2:* $200,000 + $1,493,150 − $0 = $216,800 projected retained earnings

[7]Retained earnings at the *beginning* of Year-2 is the $200,000 actual amount reported in the balance sheet at the *end* of the *current year.* Likewise, retained earnings at the *beginning* of Year-3 is the $216,800 projected amount reported at the *end* of Year-2. The $125,000 dividend in Year-3 is from the input summary data presented in Figure 5.1.

- *Year-3:* \$216,800 + \$60,734 – \$125,000 = \$161,534 projected retained earnings.

Cash

Thus far, the computation of every balance sheet forecast has been explained *except cash.* The cash projections in the Year-2 and Year-3 balance sheets could easily have been derived as *plug* figures required to balance the accounting equation (A = L + E). By rearranging this equation slightly, cash could have been computed as follows:

Liabilities + Shareholders' Equity – All Noncash Assets = Projected Cash

Using this approach, the projected cash amounts reported in the Figure 5.3 balance sheets are[8]:

- *Year-2:* \$476,350 + \$1,016,800 – \$1,473,467 = \$19,683 projected cash
- *Year-3:* \$406,422 + \$961,534 – \$1,307,586 = \$60,370 projected cash.

This approach to forecasting cash is *not* advised. The reason? It does not provide any detailed information about the anticipated sources and uses of cash from operating activities, investing activities, and financing activities. To achieve this level of detail, forecasted statements of cash flow are required.

Forecasted Statements of Cash Flow

Before examining Hometown's forecasted statements of cash flow for Year-2 and Year-3, a discussion of cash flow from *operating activities* is warranted. Cash flow from operating activities can be presented using one of two approaches—the *direct method* or the *indirect method.*[9]

[8] *Noncash assets* refer to the sum total of all assets *other than cash.*

[9] The direct method is more straightforward and easier to interpret than the indirect method. Nevertheless, the nearly all corporations use the *indirect method* in the financial statements they issue to external users. There are two reasons why. First, the indirect

The direct method has been illustrated in previous chapters due to its ease of interpretation. It *conveys directly* all sources and uses of operating cash flow in a straightforward manner, similar to the following format:

Cash Collected from Customers
– Cash Paid for Inventory
– Cash Paid for Selling, General, & Administrative Expenses
– Cash Paid for Interest Expense
= Net Cash Flow Provided by Operating Activities.

The indirect method is confusing to many users due to its somewhat *convoluted* format. It is called the indirect method because it derives operating cash flow *indirectly* by making a series of adjustments to the net income figure reported in a company's income statement. The general format of the indirect method is as follows[10]:

Net Income
+ Depreciation Expense
+ Losses on Fixed Asset Disposals (or *minus* Gains)
+ Decreases in Accounts Receivable (or *minus* Increases)
+ Decreases in Inventory (or *minus* Increases)
+ Decreases in All Other Noncash Current Assets (or *minus* Increases)
+ Increases in Trade Payables (or *minus* Decreases)
+ Increases in All Other Current Liabilities (or *minus* Decreases)
= Net Cash Flow from Operating Activities.

The best way to explain *why* these adjustments to net income result in net cash flow from operating activities is to examine Hometown's forecasted statements of cash flow illustrated in Figure 5.4.

---

method is easier to prepare than the direct method. Second, even if companies choose to use the direct method, they are required to provide a supplemental schedule of operating cash flows prepared using the indirect method. If they elect to use the indirect method, they are *not* required to provide a supplemental schedule of operating cash flows using the direct method.

[10]Adjustments to net income using the indirect method are often far more complex than what is presented here; however, the general concepts underlying the conversion of net income into operating cash flow are the same.

STATEMENT OF CASH FLOWS	Current Year Actual	Year-2 Projections	Year-3 Projections
CASH FLOW FROM OPERATING ACTIVITIES			
Net Income	$ 3,500	$ 16,800	$ 69,734
Add: Depreciation	40,000	55,000	55,000
Loss on Sale of Land	-	15,000	-
Decrease (Increase) in Accounts Receivable	(44,000)	23,333	41,067
Decrease (Increase) in Inventory	(38,000)	25,200	69,813
Increase (Decrease) in Accounts Payable	10,000	12,350	(31,928)
Net Cash Flow from Operating Activities	$ (28,500)	$ 147,683	$ 203,686
CASH FLOW FROM INVESTING ACTIVITIES			
Purchased Fixtures	$ (10,000)	$ -	$ -
Sold Land	-	$ 25,000	$ -
Purchased Computer System	-	(120,000)	-
Net Cash Flow from Investing Activities	$ (10,000)	$ (95,000)	$ -
CASH FLOW FROM FINANCING ACTIVITIES			
Issued Common Stock	$ 50,000	$ -	$ -
Paid Dividends on Common Stock	-	-	(125,000)
Principle Payments on Long-Term Debt	(33,000)	(36,000)	(38,000)
Cash Flow from Financing Net Activities	$ 17,000	$ (36,000)	$ (163,000)
Net Cash Flow from All Scources	$ (21,500)	$ 16,683	$ 40,686
Add: Beginning Cash Balance	24,500	3,000	19,683
Ending Cash Balance	$ 3,000	$ 19,683	$ 60,370

Figure 5.4 Projected statements of cash flows: year-2 and year-3

Cash Flow from Operating Activities

Starting with Year-2 net income of $16,800, the first adjustment requires *adding back* the company's Year-2 depreciation expense of $55,000. Depreciation is added to net income because it will not require any future payment of cash. Depreciation is referred to as a *noncash expense,* which means that it reduces net income without reducing cash. Thus, to convert net income to operating cash flow, depreciation expense must be added back. The same treatment of depreciation expense is repeated in Year-3.

Hometown projects a $15,000 loss on the sale of land in its Year-2 income statement. The loss—in similar fashion to depreciation expense—is *added back* to net income because it will not result in any form of cash payment. In fact, the company actually expects to *receive $25,000* by selling land in Year-2, the entire amount of which is reported in the *investing activities* section of Figure 5.4. The $15,000 loss in the company's projected income statement is simply the amount by which the land's $40,000 *original cost* exceeds its projected $25,000 selling price. The loss will reduce net income without reducing cash, so it needs to be added back to convert net income to operating cash flow.[11]

Hometown's Year-2 projected accounts receivable of $256,667 in the Figure 5.3 balance sheet is $23,333 *less* than the actual $280,000 amount at the end of the current year. The anticipated $23,333 decrease is *added* to net income in Figure 5.4. A decrease in accounts receivable means that *cash collections* from credit customers during the year *exceed credit sales* reported in the income statement. These collections increase operating cash flow without increasing net income, so to convert net income to operating cash flow the decrease must be added back. Likewise, the company's $215,600 accounts receivable projection in Year-3 is $41,067 less than the $256,666 amount forecasted in Year-2. This decrease must also be added back.[12]

Hometown's Year-2 projected inventory of $184,800 in the Figure 5.3 balance sheet is $25,200 *less* than the actual $210,000 amount at the end of the current year. The $25,200 decrease is *added* to net income in Figure 5.4. A decrease in inventory means that *cost of goods sold* reported in the income statement *exceeds inventory purchases* for the year. The $25,200 amount by which cost of goods sold is expected to exceed inventory purchases will decrease net income without decreasing operating cash flow. Thus, to determine operating cash flow the $25,200 decrease must be added to net income. Likewise, the $114,987 inventory forecast in Year-3 is $69,813 less than the $184,800 Year-2 forecast. Thus, it must be added back, as well.[13]

---

[11]Had Hometown expected to sell the $40,000 parcel of land for $55,000, a $15,000 *gain* would be reported in its forecasted Year-2 income statement, and $55,000 of cash proceeds from the sale would be reported in the *investing activities* section of the statement of cash flows. A $15,000 gain would increase net income, but it would not increase *operating cash flow.* As such, it would be *subtracted* from net income in the determination of cash flow from operating activities.

[12]*Increases* in accounts receivable occur when credit sales during the year exceed cash collections from credit customers. Credit sales increase net income without increasing operating cash flow. So to convert net income to operating cash flow, increases in accounts receivable are subtracted.

[13]*Increases* in inventory occur when inventory purchases during the year exceed cost of goods sold in the income statement. These purchases potentially decrease operating cash flow without decreasing net income. So to convert net income to operating cash flow, increases in inventory need to be subtracted.

Finally, Hometown's Year-2 projected trade payables of $112,350 in the Figure 5.3 balance sheet is $12,350 *more* than the actual $100,000 amount at the end of the current year. The $12,350 increase is *added* to net income in Figure 5.4. An increase in trade payables means that *inventory purchases* during the year *exceed cash payments* to inventory vendors. The $12,350 amount by which inventory purchases are expected to exceed cash paid to vendors is not reflected in net income, so the increase must be added back.

Conversely, the projected $80,422 trade payables balance in Year-3 is $31,928 *less* than the $112,350 Year-2 amount. A *decrease* in trade payables means that *cash payments* to inventory vendors during the year *exceed inventory purchases.* The $12,350 amount by which cash payments to vendors are expected to exceed inventory purchases is not reflected in net income, so the decrease must be *subtracted.*[14]

Cash Flow from Investing Activities

In most cases, investing cash flows result from buying or selling investments in noncurrent fixed assets.[15] Figure 5.4 reveals two investing cash flow projections, both of which are anticipated in Year-2. The first is a $25,000 cash *inflow* from the sale of land. This transaction is expected to result in the $15,000 loss that was added back to net income in determining of cash flow from operating activities. The second is a $120,000 cash *outflow* for the purchase of a new computer system. Taken together, the company's projected *net* cash flow from investing activities in Year-2 is $95,000.

Cash Flow from Financing Activities

Financing cash flows result from long-term debt and equity transactions. Figure 5.4 reveals a single financing cash *outflow* in Year-2, and two

---

[14]Changes in inventory and trade payables are not mutually exclusive occurrences—both are related to inventory purchases. The indirect method automatically takes this into account.

[15]As mentioned in Chapter 2, investing cash flows also can result from buying or selling financial investments, such as stock and bonds.

financing cash *outflows* in Year-3. The anticipated cash outflow in Year-2 pertains to the $36,000 principal payment on Hometown's $400,000 long-term note payable. A similar payment of $38,000 is forecasted in Year-3.

The company's total debt service cost of $48,000 per year is allocated between the payment of principal and the payment of interest expense. The interest expense portion is considered an *operating cash flow*. The $12,000 allocated to interest expense in Year-2, and the $10,000 allocated to interest expense in Year-3, are both included in the projected *net income* figures used to forecast operating cash flows under the indirect method.

The second financing cash outflow in Year-3 is a projected $125,000 dividend to shareholders. Recall that the shareholders of McNamer Enterprises negotiated this dividend in exchange for purchasing $50,000 of additional stock in the current year. That transaction is shown in Figure 5.4 in the *current year* as a financing cash *inflow.*

Assessment of the Forecasts

Based on an assessment of Hometown's forecasts, it appears that the company's financial position, results of operations, and cash flow prospects may improve significantly over the next 2 years. Figure 5.5 provides a summary of several key assessment measures.

Hometown's total assets are expected to decrease from $1,500,000 at the end of the current year, to $1,367,956 by the end of Year-3. This is not necessarily a bad sign, given the company's goal to reduce its accounts receivable, inventory, and trade payables by bringing related turnover statistics up to industry averages by the end of Year-3.

If Hometown can achieve its goals, total liabilities also should decline from $500,000 at the end of the current year to $406,422 by the end of Year-3, causing a decrease in its debt-to-assets percentage from 33.33 percent in the current year, to 29.71 percent by the end of Year-3. Moreover, Hometown's total shareholders' equity is forecasted to decline by *only* $38,466—from $1,000,000 at the end of the current year to $961,534 by the end of Year-3—even though it intends to distribute a $125,000 dividend in Year-3.

Key Measures of Assessment	Current Year Actual	Year-2 Projections	Year-3 Projections
Total Assets	$ 1,500,000	$ 1,493,150	$ 1,367,956
Total Liabilities	500,000	476,350	406,422
Total Shareholders' Equity	1,000,000	1,016,800	961,534
Net Cash Flow from Operating Activities	$ (28,500)	$ 147,683	$ 203,686
Ending Cash Balance	3,000	19,683	60,370
Net Income	$ 3,500	$ 16,800	$ 69,734
Net Income as a Percentage of Sales	0.25%	1.09%	4.04%
Debt-to-Assets Percentage	33.33%	31.90%	29.71%
Current Ratio	4.93-to-1	4.10-to-1	4.86-1
Quick Ratio	2.83-to-1	2.46-to-1	3.43-to-1
Accounts Receivable Turnover	5 times	6 times	8 times
Inventory Turnover	4 times	5 times	9 times
Trade Payables Turnover	6 times	8 times	12 times

Figure 5.5 Forecast summary: year-2 and year-3

The company's net income is projected to grow from $3,000 in the current year to $60,370 by Year-3, and its net income as a percentage of sales is expected to grow from a current level of 0.25 percent to 4.04 percent over a two-year period. Hometown's bankers should be comforted that operating cash flows are expected to improve from a *negative* $28,500 in the current year to an impressive $203,686 in Year-3. They also should find it encouraging that the company's current ratio is expected to hold steady, whereas its quick ratio is expected to improve significantly.

Of course, impressive forecasting outcomes must always be viewed with cautious optimism. Indeed, financial forecasts are based entirely on assumptions about an uncertain future, so actual outcomes can differ significantly from expectations if key assumptions (such as anticipated sales growth, turnover estimates, or tax rates) prove invalid. Hometown's bankers have good reason to be skeptical about these extremely optimistic forecasts. As such, they will certainly require that Hometown's management provide forecasts based on a *range* of input assumptions in order to critically evaluate best-case, worst-case, and most likely outcomes. Indeed, forecasting models should always be designed to enable comparative analyses in response to changes in key input variables.

Summary

This chapter was devoted entirely to long-term financial forecasting. It marked a shift in focus from measuring historical performance to predicting future performance. Both internal and external users of financial information routinely engage in long-term forecasting. In addition to being well versed in economic trends and industry norms, both user groups need a solid understanding of financial statement integration, accrual and deferral timing differences, and various measures of liquidity and profitability.

Chapter 6 is devoted entirely to short-term financial forecasting. Short-term financial forecasting or operational budgeting is exclusively a managerial activity. Nevertheless, the process requires the same skill set and a similar understanding of important financial statement relationships as long-term forecasting. Regardless of its time horizon, financial forecasting is an interactive and dynamic process. As such, all of the long-term forecasts illustrated throughout this chapter were prepared using *Excel.* A basic level of spreadsheet proficiency is a mandatory skill for all serious users of financial information.

CHAPTER 6

Operating Budgets

Chapter 5 illustrated long-term financial forecasts covering multiple years. Both internal and external decision makers engage in long-term forecasting. This chapter illustrates the process of *short-term* financial forecasting—an activity engaged in exclusively by internal decision makers to prepare *operating budgets*. Unlike long-term forecasts, operating budgets generally cover time horizons of less than a year—usually months or quarters.

Operating budgets are valuable *planning tools* that help managers avoid cash flow problems, anticipate financing needs, manage working capital, adjust staffing levels, develop tax strategies, and more effectively perform a variety of other important functions. They are referred to as operating budgets because they focus upon recurring operating activities, such as monitoring accounts receivable collections, coordinating payments to creditors, developing production schedules, controlling inventory levels, complying with tax-filing requirements, and managing short-term credit arrangements.

A complete operating budget consists of an integrated set of related forecasts that include, but certainly are not limited to, the following:

- Sales budgets;
- Operating expense budgets;
- Accounts receivable budgets;
- Inventory budgets;
- Trade payable budgets;
- Taxes payable budgets;
- Financing budgets;
- Capital expenditure budgets.

Together, these individual budgetary projections enable managers to prepare:

- Income statement budgets;
- Balance sheet budgets;
- Cash budgets.[1]

Designing an operating budget can be a complex endeavor for which numerous approaches are used. Even the simplest approaches must be dynamic and interactive so that projections can be adjusted efficiently as assumptions about the future change. To that end, operating budgets are always prepared using Excel or budgeting software applications.

The operating budget process illustrated in the remainder of this chapter centers on a hypothetical company called *Hopping Helga*. The illustration is fairly simple and straightforward, yet it is rigorous enough to convey the potential complexities that underlie this important activity.

The Case of Hopping Helga

Hopping Helga is a wholesale distributor of hops used for brewing beer. The company buys its product directly from growers and sells it to microbreweries throughout the Pacific Northwest. In early January of the current year, information was gathered to prepare a quarterly operating budget for January, February, and March.

December's sales in the previous year were $800,000, and they are budgeted to increase by 5 percent in January, by another 8 percent in February, and by another 10 percent in March. Cost of goods sold and gross profit as percentages of sales are expected to hold steady throughout the first quarter at 70 percent and 30 percent, respectively.

Microbrewery production increases significantly as the weather gets warmer, so Helga's sales volume always spikes in the second and third quarter of each year. In preparation for its busy season, the company steadily increases its inventory levels throughout the first quarter by

[1]In an operating budget context, a forecasted *statement of cash flows* often takes a slightly different form referred to as a *cash budget.*

purchasing more hops from its growers each month than it sells to its customers. To that end, the cost of inventory *purchases* is budgeted to *exceed by 10 percent* the cost of inventory *sold* in January, February, and March. The company's January 1st hops inventory carried forward from the prior year is $40,000.

Selling, general, and administrative expenses (SG&A) totaled $200,000 in December, and are budgeted to remain the same each month of the first quarter. Likewise, the company's $30,000 depreciation expense on its buildings, fixtures, and equipment in December is also budgeted to remain the same throughout the first quarter. On January 1st of the current year, these fixed assets—net of all prior accumulated depreciation expense—are carried in the accounting system at $1,396,200. Land on January 1st is carried in the accounting system at $250,000. The company does not intend to invest in any new fixed assets—nor does it intend to sell any of its existing fixed assets—during the first quarter.

The company's tax rate used to compute income tax expense is 30 percent. Income tax expense will *accrue* throughout the first quarter of the current year—meaning it will appear in the budgeted monthly income statements—but it will not be *paid* until April. Taxes payable carried forward from December of the *prior year* amount to $2,000, the entire amount of which is due in *March*.

Helga has a $300,000 *line of credit* arrangement with its bank. Its *annual* interest rate is 6 percent, so its *monthly* rate is only *0.5 percent* (6 percent ÷ 12 months = 0.5 percent). Should Helga experience a temporary cash shortfall, it can borrow up to $300,000 on its line of credit without having to ask the bank for approval. The arrangement is *interest only*—meaning that the company is required only to make the monthly interest payments on its outstanding principal. The outstanding principal is paid only *once each year* on June 15th. On January 1st, the outstanding unpaid principal amount carried forward from the prior year is $100,000. In anticipation of purchasing a new refrigeration unit in April, the company plans to draw an additional $40,000 on its line of credit in early March. Helga's January 1st cash balance carried forward from the prior year is $95,500.

All of Helga's sales are on credit, and its accounts receivable remain outstanding an average of *3 months* before being collected (microbreweries are notoriously slow to pay). Accounts receivable on January 1st carried forward from the prior year total *$2,100,000*. These receivables break down as follows:

- Outstanding accounts from October sales total $600,000.
- Outstanding accounts from November sales total $700,000.
- Outstanding accounts from December sales total $800,000.

Helga's inventory on January 1st carried forward from the prior year is $40,000. All inventory purchases are made on credit, and trade payables to Helga's growers remain outstanding an average of *2 months* before being paid. Trade payables on January 1st carried forward from the prior year total $910,000. They break down as follows:

- Outstanding accounts for inventory purchased in November total $350,000.
- Outstanding accounts for inventory purchased in December total $560,000.

On January 1st of the current year, Helga's shareholders' equity includes common stock of $900,000 and retained earnings of $1,969,700. The company does not plan to issue any additional stock, nor does it intend to pay any dividends, during the first quarter. Thus, the only change to shareholders' each month of the first quarter will result from budgeted net income being added to retained earnings.

The sequence of steps necessary to prepare Helga's operating budget for the first quarter of the current year is discussed in the remainder of this chapter. Bear in mind that all of the information was processed using *Excel*. Any attempt to prepare operating budgets by hand is an exercise in futility.

Sales Budgets

The first step in preparing an operating budget is to create a sales forecast because sales influence so many aspects of financial planning—including inventory requirements, accounts receivable collections, tax payments, and cost of goods sold estimates. It is essential that sales projections be derived thoughtfully by factoring in past trends, general economic conditions, and the competitive environment. Helga's sales budget for the first quarter of the current year is illustrated in Figure 6.1.

As shown in Figure 6.1, January sales of $840,000 are budgeted to exceed the current year's December sales by 5 percent ($800,000 × 105% = $840,000), and February sales of $907,200 are budgeted to exceed January sales by 8 percent ($840,000 × 108% = $907,200). Likewise, March sales of $997,920 are budgeted to exceed February's sales by 10 percent ($907,200 × 110% = $997,920).

Sales Budgets	January	February	March
Previous Month's Sales	$ 800,000	$ 840,000	$ 907,200
Sales as a % of Previous Month's Sales	105%	108%	110%
Budgeted Sales	$ 840,000	$ 907,200	$ 997,920

Figure 6.1 Sales budgets: first quarter

Selling, General, & Administrative Expense Budgets

SG&A expenses include sales commissions, marketing costs, insurance premiums, office supplies, utilities, payroll, accounting services, and legal fees.[2] Helga's SG&A expense budget for the first quarter of the current year is illustrated in Figure 6.2.

As mentioned previously, the actual SG&A expense of $200,000 incurred in December is not expected to change throughout the first quarter. As such, the monthly SG&A expense budgeted for January, February, and March is expected to remain constant at $200,000.

Budgeted SG&A Expenses	January	February	March
Previous Month's SG&A	$ 200,000	$ 200,000	$ 200,000
SG&A as a % of Previous Month's SG&A	100%	100%	100%
Budgeted SG&A Expenses	$ 200,000	$ 200,000	$ 200,000

Figure 6.2 SG&A expense budgets: first quarter

[2]SG&A costs are sometimes referred to as *operating expenses*. SG&A estimates are prepared from separate forecasts submitted by multiple offices and departments throughout the company, including the Marketing Department, Human Resources, the Accounting Department, and the Payroll Office.

Line of Credit Financing Budget	January	February	March
Beginning Line of Credit Balance	$ 100,000	$ 100,000	$ 100,000
New Line of Credit Borrowing	-	$ -	40,000
Budgeted Ending Line of Credit Balance	$ 100,000	$ 100,000	$ 140,000
Monthly Interest Rate	0.5%	0.5%	0.5%
Budgeted Interest Expense	$ 500	$ 500	$ 700

Figure 6.3 Financing budgets: first quarter

Financing Budgets

Helga's only anticipated financing activity in the first quarter of the current year is related to its line of credit with the bank. As illustrated in Figure 6.3, the *actual* line of credit balance carried forward from December is $100,000, and no new borrowing is anticipated until early March.

As discussed previously, no principal payments are due until June; however, Helga is required to pay *interest expense* each month on outstanding principal amount. At a monthly interest rate of 0.5 percent, the company's budgeted interest expense in January and February is $500 ($100,000 × 0.5% = $500). An additional $40,000 draw on the line of credit is planned in early March, so budgeted interest expense in the third month of the quarter is $700 ($140,000 × 0.5% = $700).

Income Statement Budgets

Helga's income statement budgets are illustrated in Figure 6.4. The sales amounts were taken from the sales budgets in Figure 6.1, of which cost of goods sold is budgeted at 70 percent. The SG&A expenses came from the SG&A expense budget in Figure 6.2, whereas the interest expense

Income Statement Budgets	January	February	March
Sales (Figure 6.1)	$ 840,000	$ 907,200	$ 997,920
Cost of Goods Sold (70% of Sales)	588,000	635,040	698,544
Gross Profit	$ 252,000	$ 272,160	$ 299,376
SG&A Expenses (Figure 6.2)	200,000	200,000	200,000
Depreciation Expense	30,000	30,000	30,000
Earnings Before Interest & Taxes	$ 22,000	$ 42,160	$ 69,376
Interest Expense (Figure 6.3)	500	500	700
Income Before Taxes	$ 21,500	$ 41,660	$ 68,676
Income Tax Expense (30% Average Rate)	6,450	12,498	20,603
Net Income	$ 15,050	$ 29,162	$ 48,073

Figure 6.4 Income statement budgets: first quarter

amounts came from the financing budgets in Figure 6.3. Its average tax rate used to forecast income tax expense is 30 percent.

Based on these projections, it appears that Helga is expecting a very profitable first quarter. Compared to its budgeted net income in January net income is expected to nearly double in February, even though February sales are budgeted to increase by just 8 percent. Net income in March is expected to be 67 percent higher than February's net income, even though sales in March are budgeted to increase by just 10 percent. The main reason that Helga's net income is expected to increase at a faster rate than sales is because the company has a rather high degree of *operating leverage*. Operating leverage refers to a company's *cost structure*. A company's degree of operating leverage is a measure of the extent to which expenses in the income statement are *fixed amounts* that do not change as sales levels increase or decrease.

Companies with high levels of fixed costs have high degrees of operating leverage, meaning that percentage changes in their net income can be significantly greater than the percentage changes in their sales. Helga's depreciation expense and most of its SG&A expenses are fixed costs that contribute to its relatively high degree of operating leverage.[3]

Accounts Receivable Budgets

Accounts receivable budgets help companies manage their cash flow when timing differences exist between the reporting of revenue in the income statement and the ultimate collection of cash from its customers. Helga's accounts receivable budget is illustrated in Figure 6.5.

Accounts Receivable Budgets	January	February	March
Beginning Accounts Receivable	$ 2,100,000	$ 2,340,000	$ 2,547,200
Sales (Figure 6.1)	840,000	907,200	997,920
Collections from Customers	(600,000)	(700,000)	(800,000)
Budgeted Ending Accounts Receivable	$ 2,340,000	$ 2,547,200	$ 2,745,120

Figure 6.5 Accounts receivable budgets: first quarter

[3]A company's cost structure influences breakeven points and profitability. Cost structure issues are discussed in Chapter 7.

The $2,100,000 balance on January 1st was carried forward from the prior year, and it comprises outstanding account balances for sales made in October, November, and December. All of Helga's sales are made on credit, so the sales amounts reported in the Figure 6.1 sales budgets are added to the beginning accounts receivable balances each month. The company's accounts receivable remain outstanding for an average of 3 months, so budgeted collections in January ($600,000) are from October sales, budgeted collections in February ($700,000) are from November sales, and budgeted collections in March ($800,000) are from December sales.[4]

Helga's accounts receivable are projected to grow at approximately the same rate as its sales. This makes sense, given its *annual* accounts receivable turnover rate of 4 times is expected to remain constant throughout the first quarter of the current year.[5] If this rate were to *decrease*, accounts receivable would grow more quickly than the company's sales; conversely, if the turnover rate were to *increase*, sales would grow more quickly than its accounts receivable.

Inventory Budgets

Helga's inventory budgets are presented in Figure 6.6. January's beginning inventory balance is the actual balance carried forward from December. Beginning inventory in February is the budgeted ending inventory in

Inventory Budgets	January	February	March
Beginning Inventory	$ 40,000	$ 98,800	$ 162,304
Cost of Goods Sold (Figure 6.4)	(588,000)	(635,040)	(698,544)
Purchases (Cost of Goods Sold x 110%)	646,800	698,544	768,398
Budgeted Ending Inventory	$ 98,800	$ 162,304	$ 232,158

Figure 6.6 Inventory budgets: first quarter

[4]Most companies prepare detailed *aging schedules* of their accounts receivable that enable them to more accurately forecast cash collections. Moreover, most companies reduce their receivables by an estimated amount of uncollectible accounts.

[5]Helga's receivables remain outstanding approximately three months. Thus, its turnover rate is approximately four times (12 months ÷ 3 months = 4 times).

January. Likewise, the beginning inventory in March is the budgeted ending inventory in February.

Inventory levels go down as Helga sells hops to microbreweries, and they go up when the company purchases hops from growers. Thus, the beginning inventory balance is *reduced* each month by *cost of goods sold* reported in the Figure 6.4 budgeted income statements, and it is *increased* each month by the budgeted amount hops that the company intends to *purchase*.

Recall that Helga desires to increase its inventory levels each month of the first quarter in anticipation of high demand in the second and third quarters. To do so, the company anticipates that inventory purchases will be *110 percent* of each month's budgeted cost of goods sold.[6] As a result, inventory levels will increase, as desired.

Trade Payables Budgets

Helga's trade payables budgets are presented in Figure 6.7. January's beginning balance is the actual balance carried forward from December. The beginning balance in February is the budgeted ending balance in January, whereas beginning balance in March is the budgeted ending balance in February.

Helga purchases all of its hops on credit, so budgeted purchases from the Figure 6.6 inventory budget are simply added to the beginning trade payables balances each month. The company's trade payables remain

Trade Payables Budgets	January	February	March
Beginning Trade Payables	$ 910,000	$ 1,206,800	$ 1,345,344
Purchases (Figure 6.6)	646,800	698,544	768,398
Payments	(350,000)	(560,000)	(646,800)
Budgeted Ending Trade Payables	$ 1,206,800	$ 1,345,344	$ 1,466,942

Figure 6.7 Trade payables budgets: first quarter

[6]Budgeting inventory for *manufacturing* companies is more difficult than it is for wholesalers and retailers. Manufactures do not *purchase* their inventory in ready-to-sell condition. Rather, they *create* inventory from raw materials. The inventories and cost of goods sold reported in the financial statements of manufacturing companies are composed of material costs, labor costs, and various overhead costs.

outstanding an average of 2 months, so budgeted payments in January ($350,000) are for purchases made in November, whereas budgeted payments in February ($560,000) are for purchases made in December. Budgeted payments in March ($646,800) are for the *budgeted* purchases that Helga intends to make in January.[7]

Taxes Payable Budgets

Taxes payable increase as a company *accrues* income tax expense.[8] Taxes payable go down when it *pays* income tax expenses accrued previously. Helga's taxes payable budget is illustrated in Figure 6.8.

Taxes Payable Budgets	January	February	March
Beginning Taxes Payable	$ 2,000	$ 8,450	$ 20,948
Income Tax Expense (Figure 6.4)	6,450	12,498	20,603
Income Tax Payments	-	-	(2,000)
Budgeted Ending Taxes Payable	8,450	20,948	39,551

Figure 6.8 Taxes payable budgets: first quarter

The $2,000 beginning balance in January is the actual amount carried forward from December for income tax expenses that Helga accrued—but did not pay—in the previous year. The entire $2,000 amount is due in March. This is the only income tax payment that the company will make in the first quarter. The income tax expenses reported in the budgeted income statements in Figure 6.4 are not due until April.

Cash Budgets

Helga's cash budgets for the first quarter of the current year are illustrated in Figure 6.9. The $95,500 beginning balance on January 1st is the actual amount carried forward from December of the previous year. February's

[7]Most companies prepare detailed *aging schedules* of their trade payables that enable them to more accurately forecast cash disbursements, and to more effectively take advantage of purchase discounts offered by vendors for prompt payment.

[8]*Accrued* taxes are tax expenses that are reported in the income statement before being paid.

Cash Budgets		January		February		March
Beginning Cash	$	95,500		145,000		84,500
Add:						
Collections (Figure 6.5)		600,000		700,000		800,000
Less:						
Payments of Trade Payables (Figure 6.7)		(350,000)		(560,000)		(646,800)
SG&A Expenses (Figure 6.2)		(200,000)		(200,000)		(200,000)
Payment of Taxes Payable (Figure 6.8)		-		-		(2,000)
Cash Before Borrowiing	$	145,500	$	85,000	$	35,700
Add: Line of Credit Borrowing (Figure 6.3)		-		-		40,000
Less: Interest on Line of Credit (Figure 6.3)		(500)		(500)		(700)
Ending Cash Balance	$	145,000	$	84,500	$	75,000

Figure 6.9 Cash budgets: first quarter

beginning balance is January's budgeted ending balance, whereas March's beginning balance is the ending cash balance budgeted for February.

All of Helga's forecasted cash flow activities are taken directly from five of its supporting budgets prepared previously. Cash collections are reported in the Figure 6.5 accounts receivable budgets, whereas payments of trade payables are reported in the Figure 6.7 trade payables budgets. SG&A payments are reported in the Figure 6.2 SG&A expense budgets and income tax payments are reported in the Figure 6.8 taxes payable budgets.

Budgeted financing cash flows from credit line borrowing and interest expense payments are reported in the Figure 6.3 financing budgets. Had Helga's first quarter forecasts included any investing activities—such as acquiring buildings, equipment, or land—*capital expenditures budgets* would have been prepared from which related cash flows in the company's cash budgets would have been taken. Capital expenditure topics are addressed in Chapter 8.

Notice that Helga's cash is expected to decline from $145,000 at the end of January, to just $75,000 by the end of the first quarter. Although this trend is potentially troubling, it should subside in the second quarter as cash collections from customers reported in the Figure 6.5 accounts receivable budgets are collected.

Balance Sheet Budgets

Helga's balance sheet forecasts are illustrated in Figure 6.10. Overall, the company's total assets are expected to increase by nearly 10 percent in just

Balance Sheet Budgets	January	February	March
ASSETS			
Cash (Figure 6.9)	$ 145,000	$ 84,500	$ 75,000
Accounts Receivable (Figure 6.5)	2,340,000	2,547,200	2,745,120
Inventory (Figure 6.6)	98,800	162,304	232,158
Total Current Assets	$ 2,583,800	$ 2,794,004	$ 3,052,278
Buildings, Fixtures & Equipment (Net)	1,366,200	1,336,200	1,306,200
Land	250,000	250,000	250,000
Total Noncurrent Assets	$ 1,616,200	$ 1,586,200	$ 1,556,200
Total Assets	$ 4,200,000	$ 4,380,204	$ 4,608,478
LIABIITIES			
Trade Payables (Figure 6.7)	$ 1,206,800	$ 1,345,344	$ 1,466,942
Income Taxes Payable (Figure 6.8)	8,450	20,948	39,551
Line of Credit Payable (Figure 6.3)	100,000	100,000	140,000
Total Liabilities (All Current)	$ 1,315,250	$ 1,466,292	$ 1,646,493
SHAREHOLDERS' EQUITY			
Common Stock	$ 900,000	$ 900,000	$ 900,000
Beginning Retained Earnings	1,969,700	1,984,750	2,013,912
Add: Income (Figure 6.4)	15,050	29,162	48,073
Ending Retained Earnings	$ 1,984,750	$ 2,013,912	$ 2,061,985
Shareholders' Equity	$ 2,884,750	$ 2,913,912	$ 2,961,985
Total Liabilities & Shareholders' Equity	$ 4,200,000	$ 4,380,204	$ 4,608,478

Figure 6.10 Balance sheet budgets: first quarter

2 months, from $4,200,000 at the end of January to $4,608,478 by the end of March. During this period its liabilities are expected to increase by approximately 25 percent, from $1,315,250 at the end of January to $1,646,493 by the end of March, and its shareholders' equity is expected to increase by approximately 2.7 percent, from $2,884,750 at the end of January to $2,961,985 at the end of March.[9] The projected changes in the individual balance sheet accounts are discussed next.

Total Assets

Anticipated changes in Helga's current assets are taken from three supporting budgets prepared previously. The cash balances are reported in the

[9]These percentage growth rates are for *two months* only—from the end of January to the end of March. To express them as *annual percentage rates*, they need to be multiplied by six. For instance, Helga's 2.7 percent increase in shareholders' equity is equivalent to an annualized growth rate of 16.7 percent.

Figure 6.9 cash budgets, accounts receivable are reported in the Figure 6.5 accounts receivable budgets, and inventory amounts are reported in the Figure 6.6 inventory budgets.

The company did not budget any purchases or sales of depreciable fixed assets in the first quarter. Thus, its forecast for buildings, fixtures, and equipment each month is simply the previous month's ending balance, minus the $30,000 depreciation expense reported in the Figure 6.4 income statement budgets. The depreciable asset amount carried forward at the end of December—net of accumulated depreciation—was $1,396,200, so the budgeted amount reported at the end of January is $1,366,200 ($1,396,200 minus depreciation of $30,000). The $1,336,200 February figure is $30,000 less than the January amount, whereas the $1,306,200 March figure is $30,000 less than the February amount. No changes to land were anticipated in the first quarter, so the $250,000 actual amount carried forward from December is held constant each month.[10]

Total Liabilities

Helga has no long-term liabilities, so all of its liabilities are classified as current.[11] The forecasts for its three liabilities were determined previously. The trade payables amounts are reported in the Figure 6.7 trade payables budgets. The income taxes payable amounts are reported in the Figure 6.8 taxes payable budgets, and the outstanding principal obligations on its line of credit are reported in the Figure 6.3 financing budgets.

Shareholders' Equity

Helga's $900,000 common stock figure reported in January is the actual amount carried forward from December. No additional stock issues are expected in the first quarter, so the $900,000 amount is held constant in February and March. The company does not anticipate paying any

[10]Land is not depreciated due to its unlimited useful life.

[11]The company's trade payables are paid approximately every two months, its income taxes are paid on a regular basis throughout the year, and its outstanding line of credit balance is paid in full annually on June 15th.

dividends in the first quarter, so the change in retained earnings each month results from net income reported in the Figure 6.4 budgeted income statements.

Summary

This chapter illustrated short-term financial forecasting methods used exclusively by managers to prepare operating budgets. Operating budgets generally cover time horizons of less than one year. In this chapter, they were illustrated on a monthly basis spanning one quarter. Companies often prepare monthly operating budgets spanning an entire year. With each passing month, budgetary forecasts are updated and rolled forward for another 12 months.

Operating budgets are valuable planning tools that help managers monitor and control activities related to:

- Cash flow;
- Credit policies;
- Inventory levels;
- Financial obligations coming due;
- Fixed asset investment decisions;
- Financing requirements;
- Staffing needs;
- Tax strategies.

Designing an operating budget can be a complex endeavor, but even the simplest approaches must be dynamic and interactive so that forecasts can be adjusted efficiently as assumptions about the future change.

CHAPTER 7

Cost–Volume–Profit Relationships

This chapter examines how a company's *cost structure* impacts its profitability as various activities that drive cost change in volume. The process by which these relationships are examined is referred to as cost–volume–profit analysis, or *CVP analysis.*

The term *cost structure* pertains to how a company's total costs are divided between costs that are *fixed* (those that *do not* change significantly as business activities change), and costs that are variable (those that *do* change measurably as business activities change). CVP analysis focuses upon business activities that are highly correlated with driving up a company's costs and identifies these activities as *cost drivers.* Throughout this chapter, *units produced and sold* will be the primary cost driver used to illustrate CVP relationships.[1]

CVP analysis is a valuable planning tool that can be used by managers to address questions related to:

- The number of units a company must sell in order to break even;
- The dollar amount of sales needed to achieve a target level of income;

---

[1]Many different kinds of activities can be cost drivers. For instance, in large-scale manufacturing operations, *machine hours* are often correlated highly with cost incurrence, whereas in small companies that create handcrafted products—such as custom furniture—*labor hours* can be a significant cost driver. In the airline industry, the number of *passenger miles flown* is commonly considered a primary cost driver, and in hospitals, the number of *inpatient-days* is widely used. Many companies use *multiple* cost drivers when performing CVP analysis; moreover, they apply CVP at various organizational levels including divisions, departments, and individual products.

- The amount by which current sales levels can decline before a company becomes unprofitable;
- The amount by which a company's profitability will change if its current sales mix changes, and so on.

Cost Behaviors

CVP analysis requires that managers classify costs as being either *variable* or *fixed*.[2] Variable costs vary in *total* as business activity varies, but on a *per unit* basis, they remain fixed. For instance, if the cost of producing a product includes $10 per unit in raw material, total material costs increase as the number of units produced increases; however, the material cost per unit remains fixed at $10.[3] The graphs in Figure 7.1 illustrate variable cost behavior.

Fixed cost behavior is the mirror image of variable cost behavior. Fixed costs are generally fixed in *total* across a normal range of activity, but vary *per unit* as activity varies. For example, assume that a company's monthly fixed costs remain relatively constant at $5,000 across a normal range of production activity between 1,000 units and 5,000 units. So, if 1,000 units are produced, the average fixed cost per unit will be *$5* ($5,000 ÷ 1,000 units), but if 5,000 units are produced, the average fixed cost per unit will be just *$1* ($5,000 ÷ 5,000 units). Thus, fixed costs could be as high as $5 per unit or as low as $1 per unit, which demonstrates that assigning fixed costs to products or services on a per unit basis is like trying to measure the cost of something using a rubber ruler. Consequently, CVP analysis always considers fixed costs in the *aggregate* to avoid having unit costs vary as output activity varies. The graphs in Figure 7.2 illustrate fixed cost behavior.

---

[2]Some costs are *semivariable*—or *mixed*—meaning that they contain both variable and fixed elements. For instance, electricity costs are usually composed of a fixed monthly rate plus a variable amount based on the number of kilowatt hours used.

[3]CVP analysis applies to *normal* ranges of activity. Should activities—such as production levels—fall outside of normal ranges, variable costs per unit can change as economies of scale change. If activity falls below normal, economies of scale can be lost, causing variable costs per unit to increase. Likewise, if activity exceeds what is normal, economies of scale can be gained, causing variable costs per unit to decrease.

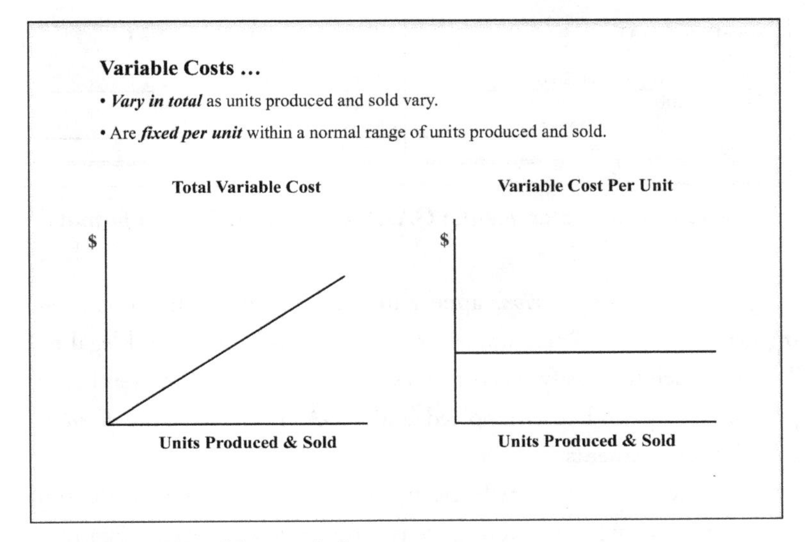

Figure 7.1 Variable cost behavior

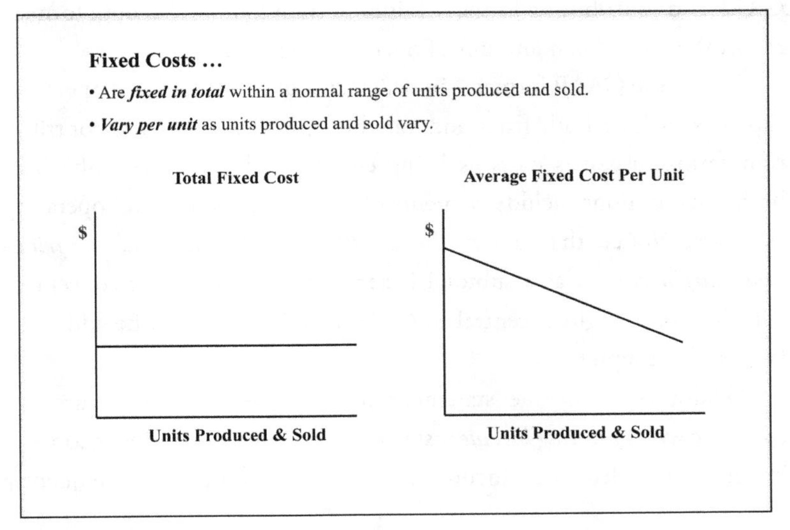

Figure 7.2 Fixed cost behavior

Contribution Income Statements

Income statements prepared for external users under generally accepted accounting principles (GAAP) assign costs and expenses to both *products* and *reporting periods.* Costs assigned to products are reported in the income statement as *cost of goods sold,* whereas costs that are more broadly

GAAP FORMAT	CONTRIBUTION FORMAT
Sales	Sales
Less: Cost of Goods Sold	Less: Total Variable Costs
Gross Profit	Total Contribution Margin
Less: Operating Expenses	Less: Total Fixed Costs
= Operating Income	= Operating Income

Figure 7.3 Income statements: GAAP versus contribution formats

assigned to *reporting periods* appear in the income statement as *operating expenses*—such as salaries, insurance, marketing costs, and legal fees. This approach to classifying costs does not work for CVP analysis because product and period costs reported under GAAP include both *fixed* and *variable* cost elements.[4]

For internal (managerial) purposes, income statements are often rearranged into what is referred to as a *contribution format.*[5] Figure 7.3 provides a side-by-side illustration of income statements prepared under GAAP and contribution formats. It is important to note that both formats report the same dollar amount of operating income.[6]

Unlike the GAAP format—in which cost of goods sold and operating expenses include both fixed and variable cost elements—the contribution format classifies costs as being either variable or fixed, of which both classifications include elements of cost of goods sold and operating expenses. Notice that under the contribution format *total contribution margin* is used as a subtotal instead of *gross profit.* The concept of contribution margin is central to CVP analysis and it will be addressed later in this chapter.

Finally, both income statement formats presented in Figure 7.3 conclude with *operating income* instead of *net income.* Operating income—income before deducting income tax expenses—is used more frequently

---

[4]This is especially true of manufacturing environments, where cost of goods sold includes large amounts of fixed overhead costs incurred in the production process.

[5]Income statements prepared under the contribution format are also referred to as *variable costing* income statements.

[6]In manufacturing environments, operating income can differ between the two formats if a company's ending inventory differs materially from its beginning inventory. The difference stems from the manner in which fixed manufacturing costs are accounted for under GAAP—a topic beyond the scope of this book.

in CVP analysis than net income because income taxes behave neither like variable costs nor like fixed costs. Income taxes are *legislated,* so they often behave in ways that defy logic.[7]

The Cost–Volume–Profit Graph

It is helpful to graph the elements of CVP relationships before engaging in the process of CVP analysis. Figure 7.4 illustrates these important CVP relationships.

The *horizontal axis* of the graph represents the number of units that a company produces and sells, whereas the *vertical axis* is expressed in dollars.[8] The *total fixed cost* line is parallel to the horizontal axis, indicating that total

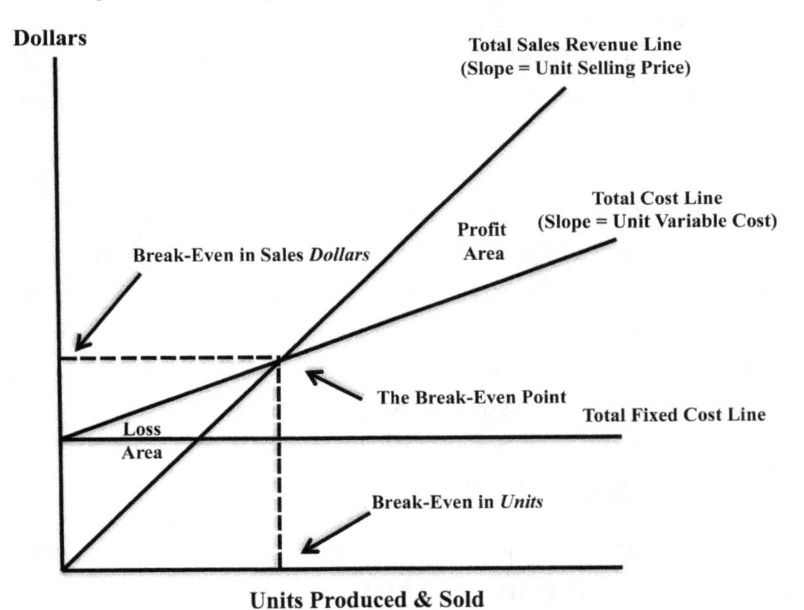

Figure 7.4 Cost–volume–profit relationships

---

[7]Using after-tax income in CVP analysis will be illustrated later in this chapter.

[8]Labeling the horizontal axis as *units produced and sold* suggests that the graph is for a manufacturing company. A wholesaler or retailer might label the horizontal axis as *units sold.* The horizontal axis used in a CVP graph needs to be a business activity that is highly correlated with a company's total cost. As discussed previously, business activities that are highly correlated with costs are called *cost drivers.* Depending on the type of business being analyzed, cost drivers might also include machine hours, labor hours, passenger miles traveled, inpatient days, and so on.

fixed costs *remain constant* over a normal range of units produced and sold. The *total cost* line is composed of fixed costs *plus* variable costs. It originates where the total fixed cost line meets the vertical axis. Hypothetically, with no production or sales activity, variable costs would be zero, and total costs would simply be a company's total fixed costs. With each additional unit produced and sold, a company's total cost goes up by the *variable cost per unit*—which means that the *slope* of the total cost line equals the variable cost per unit. Thus, the formula for total cost line can be expressed as follows:

$$\text{Total Costs} = \text{Total Fixed Costs} + (\text{Units Produced \& Sold} \times \text{Variable Cost per Unit})$$

The *total sales revenue* line begins at the graph's origin, and with each additional unit produced and sold, total sales revenue increases by the selling price per unit. Thus, the *slope* of the total sales revenue line equals the *selling price per unit.*

Initially, the graph's total cost line is above the total sales revenue line, meaning that the company is *unprofitable* and operating at a *loss.* Where the total cost and total sales revenue lines intersect is the *breakeven point* (which is measured in *sales dollars* on the vertical axis and in *units produced and sold* on the horizontal axis). At the breakeven point the company's income equals *zero.* Beyond the breakeven point, the graph's total sales revenue line is above the total cost line, meaning that the company is operating at a profit.

Contribution Margin Per Unit

The amount by which the slope of the total sales revenue line (selling price per unit) exceeds the slope of the total cost line (variable cost per unit) is referred to as the *contribution margin per unit.* Thus, the contribution margin per unit is computed as follows:

$$\text{Contribution Margin/Unit} = \text{Unit Selling Price} - \text{Unit Variable Cost}$$

Assume, for example, that a company makes a single product with a selling price of $100 and a variable cost per unit of $60. Thus, its contribution margin per unit is $40. This means that up to the breakeven point each unit produced and sold *contributes $40* toward covering the company's total *fixed costs.* After the breakeven point, each unit produced and sold *contributes $40* to the company's *operating income.* If the company's monthly fixed costs total $6,000, it must produce and sell *150 units* to break even, computed as follows:

$6,000 total fixed costs ÷ $40 contribution margin per unit
= 150 units to breakeven

It is not uncommon to express the contribution margin per unit as a *percentage* of the *selling price* per unit. The result is referred to as the *contribution margin percentage.* If the selling price is $100, and its contribution margin *per unit* is $40, then its contribution margin percentage is *40 percent,* computed as follows:

$40 contribution margin per unit ÷ $100 unit selling price
= 40% contribution margin percentage

CVP Formulas

The contribution margin per unit and the contribution margin percentage are key variables in two CVP formulas used to determine the level of sales activity required—in *units* or in *dollars*—to achieve a target level of operating income. The two formulas are provided in Figure 7.5. The manner in which these formulas are used is illustrated throughout the remainder of this chapter.

$$\text{Sales Volume (in } \textit{Units}\text{)} = \frac{\text{Fixed Costs + Target Operating Income}}{\text{Contribution Margin } \textit{Per Unit}}$$

$$\text{Sales Volume (in } \textit{Dollars}\text{)} = \frac{\text{Fixed Costs + Target Operating Income}}{\text{Contribution Margin } \textit{Percentage}}$$

Figure 7.5 Sales volume required for target operating income

The Case of Splash Enterprises—Part I

Splash Enterprises manufactures and sells ski vests used by water skiers and boaters. It currently sells no other products. A summary of the company's unit selling price, unit variable cost, monthly fixed costs, contribution margin, and contribution margin percentage is provided in Figure 7.6.

Using the information in Figure 7.6 with the CVP formulas in Figure 7.5 enables Splash's management team to better understand important relationships involving the company's cost structure, its volume of sales activity, and its profitability.

What Is Splash's Monthly Breakeven Point in Units?

As mentioned previously, the breakeven point is reached when a company's total sales revenue equals its total costs. At the breakeven point operating income equals *zero*. Thus, using the *first* CVP formula shown in Figure 7.5, Splash's monthly breakeven point in *units* is estimated as follows:

Sales in Units = [Fixed Costs + Target Operating Income]
÷ Contribution Margin/Unit

Sales in Units = [$270,000 + $0] ÷ $90

Sales in Units = 3,000 Units

CVP: Single Product		Ski Vests
Unit Selling Price	$	150
Unit Variable Cost		(60)
Contribution Margin *Per Unit*	$	90
Contribution Margin *Percentage*		60%
Monthly Fixed Costs	$	270,000

Figure 7.6 CVP analysis in a single product environment

In short, if Splash sells fewer than 3,000 ski vests in any given month, it will report an operating *loss*; however, each ski vest produced and sold in excess of 3,000 units will *contribute $90*—the contribution margin per unit—to the company's monthly operating income.

What Is Splash's Monthly Breakeven Point in Dollars?

Again, operating income equals *zero* at the breakeven point, so using the *second* CVP formula shown in Figure 7.5, the company's monthly breakeven point in *dollars* is estimated as follows:

Sales in *Dollars* = [Fixed Costs + Target Operating Income] ÷ Contribution Margin%

Sales in *Dollars* = [$270,000 + $0] ÷ 60%

Sales in *Dollars* = $450,000

To avoid an *operating loss,* Splash needs to generate monthly sales revenue of at least $450,000. After the breakeven point is reached, *each dollar* of sales revenue in excess of $450,000 will *contribute $0.60*—the contribution margin percentage—to the company's monthly *operating income.*[9]

It is easy to see that fixed costs directly impact a company's ability to break even. The more a company's cost structure is composed of fixed costs—relative to variable costs—the more difficult it becomes for it to break even. For instance, if Splash's fixed costs increase by *$90,000*—from $270,000 to $360,000—its level of sales required to break even will increase by *$150,000*—from $450,000 to $600,000—and its breakeven point will increase from 3,000 units to 4,000 units.[10]

---

[9]The same $450,000 breakeven sales figure could have been derived by multiplying the company's breakeven point in *units* by the selling price per ski vest: 3,000 units × $150 per ski vest = $450,000.

[10]Breakeven computations if fixed costs increase to $360,000: [$360,000 + $0] ÷ 60% = $600,000; [$360,000 + $0] ÷ $90 = 4,000 units.

Beyond the Breakeven Point

It would not make sense for a company to establish the breakeven point as its target performance objective. The breakeven point is determined simply to ascertain the sales level required (in units or in dollars) to cover total fixed costs. The more important issue that confronts managers is how *profit changes* in response to sales once the breakeven point has been reached. Understanding how cost structure affects profitability enables managers to estimate the sales volumes necessary to achieve profitability targets beyond the breakeven point.

In May, Splash's management team set a target operating income of $72,000 for June. Historically, the average operating income in June has been $63,000. How many ski vests must Splash sell to achieve its target? The answer to that question can be quickly determined using the *first* CVP formula shown in Figure 7.5:

Sales in *Units* = [Fixed Costs + Target Operating Income] ÷ Contribution Margin/Unit

Sales in *Units* = [$270,000 + $72,000] ÷ $90

Sales in *Units* = 3,800 Units

Using the *second* CVP formula shown in Figure 7.5, the *dollar* level of sales required for Splash to achieve its June target is:

Sales in *Dollars* = [Fixed Costs + Target Operating Income] ÷ Contribution Margin%

Sales in *Dollars* = [$270,000 + $72,000] ÷ 60%

Sales in *Dollars* = $570,000

Given that Splash's average operating income in June is $63,000, by how much can the company's sales revenue (in *dollars*) *decline* before it becomes *unprofitable?* CVP analysis makes the answer to this question easy to determine. Using the *second* CVP formula shown in Figure 7.5, the *dollar* level of sales required for Splash to achieve June's average operating income of $63,000 is determined as follows:

Sales in *Dollars* = [Fixed Costs + Target Operating Income] ÷ Contribution Margin%

Sales in *Dollars* = [$270,000 + $63,000] ÷ 60%

Sales in *Dollars* = $555,000

Splash's sales revenue (in dollars) required to *break even* was determined previously as $450,000. Should sales decline below this amount, the company will be unprofitable. Thus, the $555,000 average sales revenue in June can decline by $105,000 before Splash incurs an *operating loss.* The amount by which a company's current sales level can decline before it becomes unprofitable is referred to as its *margin of safety.* In this case, Splash's margin of safety is $105,000.[11]

What about Taxes?

Up to this point, CVP analysis has been illustrated using *operating income* instead of *after-tax income.* What if Splash wants to estimate sales activity to achieve a target after-tax income? Dividing the after-tax income target by *one minus the company's average tax rate,* and using that result in the Figure 7.5 formulas, enables CVP analysis to be used for after-tax estimates.

For instance, assume that Splash's average tax rate is 25 percent, and that management wants to determine the sales revenue required (in *dollars*) for an *after-tax* profit of *$45,000.* One minus the company's average tax rate of 25 percent equals *75 percent,* and $45,000 after-tax profit divided by 75 percent equals *$60,000.* Using this figure as the

[11]Splash's margin of safety also can be stated as *700 units* ($105,000 margin of safety ÷ $150 selling price per unit = 700 units). Thus, average sales in June could fall by 700 units before Splash would report a monthly operating loss.

income target in the *second* CVP formula shown in Figure 7.5, the *dollar* level of sales required for Splash to achieve an *after-tax profit of $45,000* is derived as follows:

Sales in *Dollars* = [Fixed Costs + (After-Tax Income)/(1 − Tax Rate)] ÷ Contribution Margin%

Sales in *Dollars* = [$270,000 + ($45,000/75%)] ÷ 60%

Sales in *Dollars* = [$270,000 + $60,000] ÷ 60%

Sales in *Dollars* = $550,000

As noted previously, income taxes do not behave like variable costs, nor do they behave like fixed costs. Income taxes are *legislated,* and they often behave in ways that defy logic. As such, it is common for managers to use operating income—instead of after-tax income—when performing CVP analysis.

The Case of Splash Enterprises—Part II

In the previous section, Splash produced and sold ski vests as its only product. Of course, many companies sell hundreds or even thousands of different products. So the obvious question is whether CVP analysis applies to multiple product environments. The answer to that question is *yes,* but with some adjustments. The complexity of applying CVP increases as product lines increase; however, the underlying conceptual issues of most importance are pretty much the same across an array of multiple product environments.

To illustrate, assume that Splash decides to diversify its offerings to include life vests, slalom skis, and ski ropes. Information pertaining to its expanded line of products is provided in Figure 7.7.

As indicated, the company's ski vests sell for $150 apiece, provide a contribution margin of $90 per unit, and account for approximately 70 percent of the company's total sales revenue. Slalom skis sell for $475 apiece, offer a contribution margin of $275 per unit, and account

CVP: Multiple Products	Ski Vests	Slalom Skis	Ski Ropes
Unit Selling Price	$ 150	$ 475	$ 100
Unit Variable Cost	(60)	(200)	(20)
Contribution Margin *Per Unit*	$ 90	$ 275	$ 80
Sales Mix Percentages	70%	20%	10%
Monthly Fixed Costs	$ 360,000		

Figure 7.7 CVP analysis in a multiple product environment

for 20 percent of the company's total sales revenue. Ski ropes (with all of their necessary hardware) sell for $100 apiece, have a contribution margin of $80 per unit, and account for the remaining 10 percent of the company's total sales revenue.[12] The decision to produce and sell multiple product lines increased Splash's monthly fixed costs from $270,000 to $360,000.

Now that Splash sells more than one product, expressing its sales activity in total *unit* sales is less meaningful than expressing its sales activity in total *dollars* of sales revenue. For this reason, multiproduct companies generally use CVP analysis only for determining the total *dollars* of sales revenue necessary to achieve operating income targets.

Recall that in a single product environment, determining sales levels in dollars was computed using the contribution margin *percentage* in the following CVP formula introduced in Figure 7.5:

$$\text{Sales in } \textit{Dollars} = [\text{Fixed Costs} + \text{Target Operating Income}] \div \text{Contribution Margin\%}$$

In a single product environment, the contribution margin percentage is the product's contribution margin per unit divided by its selling price per unit. In a multiproduct environment, every product has a *unique* contribution margin and selling price. Thus, determining sales levels

[12]The *sales mix percentages* shown in Figure 7.7 refer to how much each product contributes to the total sales revenue generated by the entire company. Thus, ski vests provide 70 percent of the company's total sales revenue, whereas ski ropes provide only 10 percent.

in dollars requires a *weighted-average contribution margin percentage* (WACM%). The WACM% is computed by dividing a company's *weighted-average contribution margin* (WACM) by its *weighted-average selling price* (WASP).

The computation of Splash's WACM% is provided in Figure 7.8. In the top half of Figure 7.8, Splash's WACM of *$126* was computed by multiplying each product's contribution margin by its sales mix percentage, and summing the results across all product lines. In the bottom half of Figure 7.8, the company's WASP of *$210* was computed by multiplying each product's selling price by its sales mix percentage, and summing the results across all products. Thus, Splash's WACM% (WACM ÷ WASP) is *60 percent* ($126 ÷ $210), which can be used to modify CVP formula introduced in Figure 7.5 by substituting it in the denominator, as shown below:

Sales in *Dollars* = [Fixed Costs + Target Operating Income] ÷ WACM%

Using this modified formula, CVP analysis is no more difficult than when Splash sold only life vests—assuming that its sales mix percentages remain relatively constant.

Weighted Average Contribution Margin (WACM)	**Contrubution Margin**		**Sales Mix**		**WACM**
Ski Vests	$ 90	x	70%	=	$ 63
Slalom Skis	275	x	20%	=	55
Ski Ropes	80	x	10%	=	8
WACM					**$ 126**
Weighted Average Selling Price (WASP)	**Selling Price**		**Sales Mix**		**WASP**
Ski Vests	150	x	70%	=	105
Slalom Skis	475	x	20%	=	95
Ski Ropes	100	x	10%	=	10
WASP					**$ 210**
WACM% (WACM ÷ WASP)					**60%**

Figure 7.8 Weighted-average contribution margin percentage

What Is Splash's Monthly Breakeven Point in Dollars?

At the breakeven point, operating income is *zero.* Thus, its breakeven point in *sales dollars* is:

Sales in *Dollars* = [Fixed Costs + Target Operating Income] ÷ WACM%

Sales in *Dollars* = [$360,000 + $0] ÷ 60%

Sales in *Dollars* = $600,000

So long as Splash's sales mix percentages remain relatively constant, it needs to generate monthly sales revenue of at least $600,000 to avoid an *operating loss.* Once the breakeven point is reached, each dollar of sales revenue in excess of $600,000 will contribute $0.60—the WACM%—to the company's monthly operating income.

Achieving Operating Income Targets

Assume that Splash's management has set an operating income target of $150,000 for the upcoming month. Applying the same formula that was used to determine the company's breakeven point, the *sales dollars* required to achieve its target operating income can be estimated as follows:

Sales in *Dollars* = [Fixed Costs + Target Operating Income] ÷ WACM%

Sales in *Dollars* = [$360,000 + $150,000] ÷ 60%

Sales in *Dollars* = $850,000

If this target is achieved, Splash's margin of safety—the amount by which its sales can decline before it becomes unprofitable—will be

$250,000 (the target sales revenue of $850,000, minus the breakeven sales revenue of $600,000).

Achieving After-Tax Income Targets

Had Splash's target income for the upcoming month been $180,000 expressed as an *after-tax* amount, the same approach that was used in the single product illustration can be applied. If the company's tax rate is 25 percent, the required sales in dollars can be estimated by dividing the target after-tax income by *75 percent* (one minus the tax rate), and by substituting the WACM% in the denominator, as shown below:

Sales in *Dollars* = [Fixed Costs + (After-Tax Income)/(1 − Tax Rate)] ÷ WACM%

Sales in *Dollars* = [$360,000 + ($180,000/75%)] ÷ 60%

Sales in *Dollars* = [$360,000 + $240,000] ÷ 60%

Sales in *Dollars* = $1,000,000

Managing Sales Mix Percentages

Managers often try to improve profitability by shifting the sales mix away from products with the lowest contribution margin percentages to those with the highest contribution margin percentages. This strategy is sometimes referred to as improving the *quality of sales*.

Ski vests account for 70 percent of Splash's sales revenue and have a contribution margin percentage of 60 percent ($90 per unit contribution margin ÷ $150 unit selling price). Slalom skis account for 20 percent of the company's sales revenue and have a 57.9 percent contribution margin percentage ($275 unit contribution margin ÷ $475 selling price). Thus, Splash would not benefit from efforts to shift its sales mix *away from* ski vests to sales of slalom skies. Ski ropes account for only 10 percent of the company's sales revenue; however, they generate a contribution margin percentage of 80 percent ($80 per unit contribution margin ÷ $100 selling price).

As such, Splash may wish to explore marketing efforts that would increase the percentage of its total sales revenue that it generates from ski ropes.

Summary

This chapter examined the impact of cost structure on a company's profitability as business activity changed in volume.[13] The process by which these relationships were examined was referred to as CVP analysis. Throughout the chapter CVP analysis was used to graph cost behaviors, determine breakeven points, compute sales volume needed to achieve target incomes, quantify margins of safety, and to better understand a variety of other issues related to a company's cost structure.

CVP analysis is a powerful managerial tool; however, CVP formulas are based on several fairly rigid assumptions. For instance, increases in total sales revenue and total costs are considered linear over a normal range of activity, whereas total fixed costs are assumed to remain constant as activity levels change. For companies that sell multiple product lines, sales mix percentages are assumed to be constant in the short run, and for manufacturing companies, units produced are assumed to equal units sold.

Even though CVP analysis is a fairly straightforward endeavor, even the simplest CVP models must be flexible and interactive so that inputs to the process can be adjusted efficiently as assumptions about the future change. Thus, CVP analysis is almost always performed using *Excel* or cost accounting software. In fact, CVP relationships often are built into robust forecasting models similar to those examined in Chapters 5 and 6.

[13]CVP focuses exclusively on the relationship between cost structure and *profitability;* it is not used to analyze relationships that exist between a company's cost structure and its *cash flow.*

CHAPTER 8

Capital Budgeting

This concluding chapter introduces the basic concepts and practices associated with *capital budgeting*. Capital budgets help managers evaluate and prioritize competing capital investment opportunities. Unlike recurring operating expenses—such as insurance premiums, payroll obligations, and property taxes—capital investments refer to large financial resource allocations having long-term consequences. Examples include purchases of manufacturing equipment, replacements of aircraft, launches of new product lines, and acquisitions of other companies. Once a capital investment has been made, it is difficult—if not impossible—to reverse the decision. Thus, it is essential that managers engage in rigorous analyses and make realistic projections about the potential impact of every capital investment decision.

Capital budgeting shares similarities with the long-term forecasting techniques illustrated in Chapter 5. However, the forecasts made in Chapter 5 pertained to activities of entire businesses in the *aggregate*. Moreover, the projections made in Chapter 5 culminated in a complete set of forecasted financial statements used to predict a company's profitability, solvency, and liquidity. Capital budgeting does not focus upon entire businesses in the aggregate; rather, it focuses only upon variables that are expected to change *incrementally* as a result of making a specific capital investment. In other words, capital budgeting examines how certain key variables—such as sales, expenses, net income, and working capital—are likely to change as a direct result of making a particular capital investment.[1] Forecasted changes in these key variables are used to

---

[1]Working capital refers to the composition of a company's current assets and current liabilities. Capital investments often impact a company's working capital position by causing significant changes in its accounts receivable, inventory, trade payables, and income tax accruals.

generate *cash flow* estimates required for measuring an investment's financial viability. The *payback period, net present value (NPV),* and *internal rate of return (IRR)* are the most common capital budgeting measures used to assess the desirability of a potential investment opportunity.

The Capital Budgeting Process

The only capital budgeting variable known with certainty is the initial cost of a particular investment. Everything from that point forward is based on assumptions and forecasts that span many years. Thus, the stakes are high and the potential for downside risk is considerable. Although far from foolproof, capital budgeting provides a framework for navigating these uncharted waters.

Imagine a capital investment as a $1 million *seed* with the potential to grow into a fruitful *money tree.* Once purchased, there is no turning back. The $1 million seed is planted, and additional resources are consumed each year to water and fertilize it. The seed germinates and sprouts, and over time a money tree produces an abundance of *leaves* in the form of *cash.* As the cash falls to the ground at the end of each year, it is put into large plastic bags, taken inside, and counted. After many years, the tree grows old and dies.

For the seed to be considered a good investment it must yield enough cash to recover its $1 million cost *plus* provide a *reasonable return* on investment before the money tree perishes. The capital budgeting process assesses the likelihood that the seed will germinate and be fruitful, projects how quickly the seed's $1 million cost will be *recouped,* and determines how much cash in excess of the initial $1 million investment is a *reasonable return* expectation. Figure 8.1 provides a model for conceptualizing the general framework of the capital budgeting process. A brief discussion of the model's sequential elements is necessary before providing a comprehensive illustration.

Determine the Initial Capital Investment Cost

In most circumstances, the actual cost of a capital investment is *known.* It generally includes all costs considered reasonable and necessary for

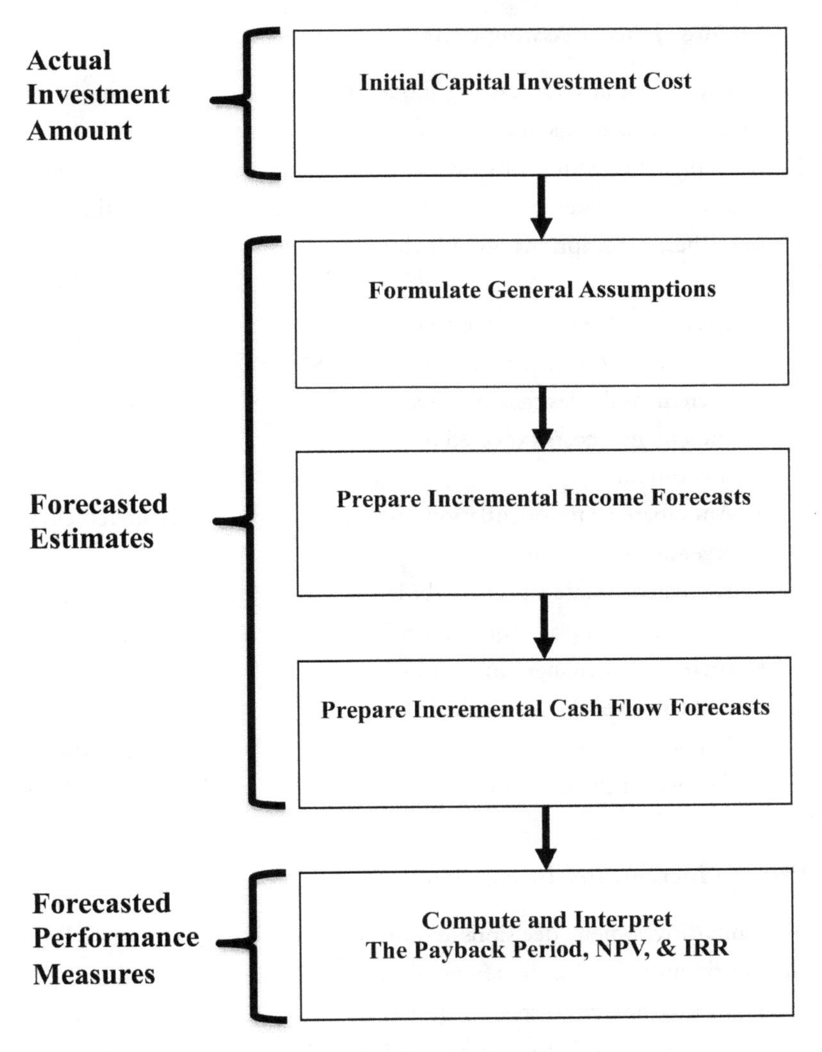

Figure 8.1 The capital budgeting process

an investment to begin serving its intended purpose. These costs typically include a negotiated acquisition price, sales taxes, delivery costs, site preparation, and training and testing costs. The initial cost of any capital investment is analogous to the $1 million seed required to grow a *money tree*.

Formulate General Assumptions

The reliability of any forecasting model depends highly on formulating reasonable expectations about the future. Perhaps the most critical step in the capital budgeting process is articulating a general set of reliable assumptions associated with a capital investment's potential financial impact. These assumptions often include the:

- Estimated life of the investment;
- Depreciation or amortization associated with the investment;
- Incremental sales that the investment is expected to generate;
- Incremental costs expected to be incurred as a result of making the investment;
- Anticipated rate of inflation and how it will impact incremental revenue and expenses;
- Estimated tax rate expected to be in effect over the life of the investment;
- Incremental debt and equity financing needed to acquire the investment;
- Incremental changes in various working capital accounts expected to occur over the life of the investment;
- Liquidation proceeds—if any—anticipated from the future sale or disposal of the investment.

Prepare Incremental Income Forecasts

All capital investment decisions require that management forecast how an investment will affect incremental income. Again, the capital budgeting process is not concerned with a company's overall performance in the *aggregate*; rather, it focuses only upon variables that are expected to change *incrementally* as a result of making a specific investment. Thus, incremental income forecasts are estimates of how a particular capital investment is expected to impact a company's income over time.

Prepare Incremental Cash Flow Forecasts

Once incremental income forecasts have been made, they are *converted* into incremental cash flow forecasts in the same way that net income was converted to cash flow from operating activities using the *indirect method* illustrated in Chapter 5. The conversion process involves adding back depreciation and adjusting net income up or down in response to anticipated changes in accounts receivable, inventory, trade payables, and other relevant accounts. Forecasting a capital investment's incremental cash flow is illustrated later in the chapter.

Compute and Interpret the Payback Period, NPV, and IRR

As mentioned previously, the payback period, NPV, and IRR are the most common capital budgeting measures used to assess desirability of a potential investment opportunity. Each of these measures is computed using *incremental cash flow* forecasts. Estimating an investment's payback period is a rather straightforward endeavor, whereas NPV and IRR require an understanding of the *time-value of money.*

The Time-Value of Money

If given an option to receive $10,000 today, or wait 5 years to receive the same amount, most rational people will opt to receive the cash sooner rather than later. The reason for their preference is that money has a *time-value*—meaning that a dollar received today is of more value to someone than a dollar to be received in the future—so the prospect of receiving $10,000 right now is more desirable than the prospect of receiving the same amount next month, next year, or 5 years from now. In fact, the longer someone must wait to receive a dollar, the *less value* they will place on the prospect of receiving it.

Money has a *time-value* because the sooner a dollar is received the more quickly it can be *invested* to generate additional dollars. If given an option to receive $9,520 today or $10,000 five years from now, most people will opt to have the lesser amount today, because by investing the $9,520 at an annual return of *just 1 percent,* it will grow to *more than* $10,000 in 5 years. However, if given an option to receive $4,020 today or $10,000 five years from now, most will opt to *wait* for the larger amount, because unless the $4,020 can be invested to earn a *minimum* annual return of *20 percent,* it will be worth *less than* $10,000 in 5 years.[2]

[2]The annual rates of return referred to in this simple illustration are compound rates, and the figures provided to not include income tax consequence.

Time-value-of-money concepts play a key role in the capital budgeting process. Managers must forecast the cash flows that a capital investment is expected to generate, estimate the timing of those cash flows, and determine the *minimum return* that an investment opportunity must yield for it to be considered acceptable. The importance of understanding time-value-of-money concepts, and how these concepts influence capital investment decisions, is illustrated in the following section.

The Case of Satka Manufacturing

Satka Manufacturing supplies the automobile industry with electrical components used in onboard GPS navigation systems. Due to an industry-wide slowdown, one of the company's production facilities is currently idle. Satka recently received a contract proposal from the Department of Defense to produce a component for a top-secret military weapon. The contract spans 4 years and requires an investment in a highly specialized piece of production equipment. Military officials will dispose of the equipment at the end of the 4-year project, and the contract guarantees Satka a $49,000 salvage value. The equipment has no alternative uses, and Satka must surrender it when the contract terminates.

To determine the viability of the proposal, Satka's required investment in the specialized production equipment will be evaluated using the capital budgeting process diagramed in Figure 8.1. Each step of the process is highlighted in the following discussion.

Initial Investment Cost

The base cost of the specialized equipment is $600,000; however, site preparation and testing procedures will cost an additional $25,000. Thus, the total cost of the investment is $625,000. If Satka agrees to accept this contract, it will purchase the equipment with its cash reserves to avoid any incremental financing costs.

General Assumptions

The contract requires the Department of Defense to pay for all orders *prior to shipment*. Thus, Satka's accounts receivable are not anticipated to change incrementally over the term of the contract. Satka will produce only the number of units specified for each order, and each order will be shipped immediately upon completion to avoid any warehousing costs. Moreover, raw material deliveries will be placed immediately into production, and all vendors will be paid within days. As such, no incremental changes to inventory levels or trade payables are anticipated over the term of the contract.

For capital budgeting purposes, the equipment's depreciation will be based on the *MACRS* method used by Satka for federal income tax purposes.[3] The depreciation deductions allowed by the Internal Revenue Code for this particular category of specialized equipment are presented in Figure 8.2. Note that each year's allowable deduction is specified as a *percentage* of the investment's initial cost.

Incremental sales over the 4-year project are projected to be $700,000 in Year-1, $800,000 in Year-2, $900,000 in Year-3, and $850,000 in Year-4. Incremental *variable* costs are expected to remain constant at *30 percent* of sales, and will consist primarily of labor, materials, and

	Initial Investment	x	MACRS Percentage	=	Annual Deduction
Year-1	$625,000	x	33%	=	$206,250
Year-2	625,000	x	44%	=	$275,000
Year-3	625,000	x	13%	=	$81,250
Year-4	625,000	x	10%	=	$62,500
			100%		**$625,000**

Figure 8.2 MACRS *depreciation deductions*

[3]MACRS—Modified Accelerated Cost Recovery System—is a depreciation method allowed *only for federal income tax purposes.* Accordingly, the use of MACRS is not permitted in the financial statements that corporations file with the SEC. Nevertheless, MACRS is frequently used for capital budgeting purposes because it directly impacts a company's income tax payments. As such, MACRS depreciation results in a more accurate estimate of an investment's after-tax incremental cash flow than depreciation methods used in the financial reports issued to external investors and creditors.

energy costs. Incremental *fixed* costs are expected to be $260,000 in the first year of the contract, and increase each year by a projected rate of *inflation of 3 percent.* Incremental fixed expenditures will be composed primarily of increased security costs, additional IT support, and higher insurance premiums. Satka's income tax rate is expected to remain constant at *40 percent* throughout the contract period.

Incremental Income Forecasts

Satka's incremental income projections are provided in Figure 8.3. These projections are consistent with the terms of the contract and management's assumptions.

At first glance, incremental income projections appear to be very strong, especially in Year-3 and Year-4. Income forecasts are much lower in Year-1 and Year-2, due to the large depreciation deductions allowed by the Internal Revenue Code in the first 2 years of the contract. Notice how much *lower* Satka's income tax projections are in the first 2 years of the project compared to the last 2 years. Being able to deduct so much of the equipment's cost so quickly, and thereby reduce income taxes so significantly, is the primary benefit of using MACRS for tax purposes.[4]

	Year 1	Year 2	Year 3	Year 4
Sales	$ 700,000	$ 800,000	$ 900,000	$ 850,000
Variable Costs	210,000	240,000	270,000	255,000
Contribution Margin	$ 490,000	$ 560,000	$ 630,000	$ 595,000
Fixed Costs	260,000	267,800	275,834	284,109
Depreciation Expense	206,250	275,000	81,250	62,500
Income Before Taxes	$ 23,750	$ 17,200	$ 272,916	$ 248,391
Income Taxes	9,500	6,880	109,166	99,356
Net Income	$ 14,250	$ 10,320	$ 163,750	$ 149,035

Assumptions:

- Variable costs are projected to remain 30% of incremental sales throughout the entire contract.
- Fixed costs of $260,000 in year-1 are expected to increase each year by a 3% rate of inflation.
- MACRS deprecation amounts are taken from **Figure 8.2.**
- The average income tax rate is forecasted to remain 40% throughout the entire contract.

Figure 8.3 Incremental income projections

[4]The time-value of money makes the immediate *tax savings* provided by MACRS depreciation extremely attractive. The more quickly a company is able to deduct the cost of a capital investment for tax purposes, the more desirable the resulting tax savings become.

	Year 1	Year 2	Year 3	Year 4
Net Income	$ 14,250	$ 10,320	$ 163,750	$ 149,035
Add: Depreciation	206,250	275,000	81,250	62,500
Add: Disposal Proceeds				49,000
Net Cash Flow	$ 220,500	$ 285,320	$ 245,000	$ 260,535

Figure 8.4 Incremental cash flow projections

Incremental Cash Flow Forecasts

The incremental cash flow projections shown in Figure 8.4 were derived by adjusting the incremental *net income* amounts computed in Figure 8.3.

As discussed previously, Satka does not anticipate any changes in its working capital accounts—accounts receivable, inventory, or trade payables—so the only required adjustments to net income are adding back annual depreciation expense, and including the equipment's $49,000 disposal proceeds at the end of the 4-year contract.[5] Notice that *net cash flows* in the first two years of the contract are *significantly greater* than the *net income projections* once the disproportionally large depreciation deductions allowed under the Internal Revenue Code are added back.

The contract's projected incremental cash flow over the 4-year period totals $1,011,354, which exceeds the required $625,000 equipment investment by $386,354. The final step of the capital budgeting process is determining whether the $386,354 net benefit is *reasonable*, given the inherent risks associated with this particular project.

As noted previously, the payback period, NPV, and IRR are the most common capital budgeting measures used to assess whether the potential benefits of an investment opportunity reasonably compensate the investor for risk. Satka's potential investment in specialized equipment will illustrate each of these capital budgeting measures.

The Payback Period

Although the incremental 4-year cash flow of Satka's contract is expected to exceed its initial investment cost by $386,354, it is important to

[5]Recall from Chapter 5 that depreciation expense is added back in determining net cash flow because, unlike most other expenses, depreciation reduces net income without reducing *cash*.

		Net Cash Flow
Year-1	$	220,500
Year-2		285,320
Net Cash Flow After Two Years	$	505,820
Year-3 Requirement		119,180
Initial Cost of Investment	$	625,000
(a) Year-3 *Requirement*	$	119,180
(b) Year-3 *Total* Forecasted Cash Flow	$	245,000
(a) ÷ (b)		0.49
Payback Period		**2.49 years**

Figure 8.5 The payback period

estimate *how quickly* the cost of the investment will be recovered. The amount of time that it takes for an investment to pay for itself is called *the payback period.* Generally speaking, once an investment's cost has been fully recovered, any unforeseen negative circumstances are potentially less damaging than when they occur before recouping the investment's cost. Thus, investments with relatively short payback periods are considered safer—less risky—than those with long payback periods.[6]

Using the incremental cash flow estimates developed in Figure 8.4, the projected payback period for Satka's required investment in specialized equipment is *2.49 years,* as illustrated in Figure 8.5.

Figure 8.5 reveals that the investment's total incremental cash flow after *two full-years* is expected to be $505,820 ($220,500 in Year-1, plus $285,320 in Year-2). Thus, only $119,180 of incremental cash flow is required in Year-3 to recover the equipment's $625,000 initial cost. If the net cash flow from this project is to be received at a constant linear rate throughout Year-3, dividing the $119,180 Year-3 requirement by Year-3's $245,000 estimated cash flow suggests that the equipment's cost will be recovered about half-way through the year ($119,180 ÷ $245,000 = 49%). Thus, its *payback period* is *2.49 years* (two full-years, plus 49 *percent* of a year).

Estimating an investment's payback period is an important part of the capital budgeting process; however, it treats all cash flows

[6]When unforeseen negative circumstances occur *prior* to the recovery of an investment's cost, the likelihood that the cost will *never* be recovered can pose a significant threat.

equally—regardless of their timing—and thereby ignores that money has a time-value. As discussed previously, Satka should take into consideration that dollars received toward the end of the contract are of less value than dollars received in earlier years.

NPV and IRR

Both NPV and IRR take the time-value of money into consideration. To compare the $625,000 investment required at the *beginning* of the contract to *cash flows* forecasted over the contract's 4-year term, future cash flows must be *discounted* by applying an appropriate *discount rate*. The discount rate used is equivalent to the *rate of return* required to compensate a company for risk. The higher the perceived risk associated with any capital investment, the more its future cash flows will be discounted, and the lower its *discounted present value* will be. The lower the perceived risk associated with a capital investment, the less its future cash flows will be discounted, and the higher its *discounted present value* will be.[7] Satka perceives that this particular project is highly risky for a variety of reasons:

- Developing components for military weapons increases the likelihood of security threats and security breaches.
- If the automobile manufacturing industry rebounds, Satka will be unable to use its production facility to fulfill increased orders for GPS components.
- Satka's board of directors is not particularly enthusiastic about the company diversifying its offerings to include components used in military weapons.

[7]Even when the perceived risk of a potential investment is very low, the discount rate used to compute the discounted present value of its future cash flows must at least equal the company's *weighted average cost of capital* (WACC). A company's WACC is a function of the cost of its debt financing and equity financing, and the relative reliance it places upon each financing method. Computing a company's WACC is beyond the scope of this book. In short, if an investment's rate of return is not high enough to offset the cost of financing it, the investment will not be profitable, nor will it increase the net *financial value* of the company.

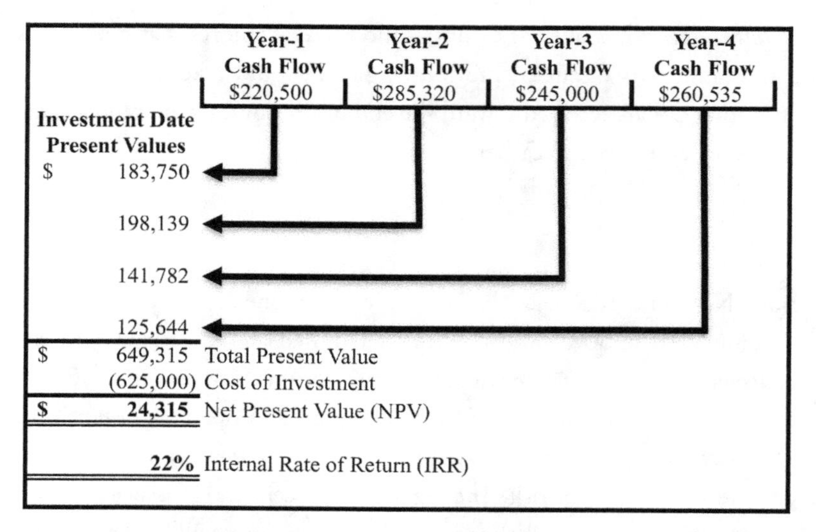

Figure 8.6 NPV & IRR: discount rate = 20%

For most capital investments, Satka's management rarely uses a discount rate in excess of 15 percent to compensate the company for risk. However, it perceives the investment risk of this particular project so great that it must have the potential to generate a minimum rate of return of *20 percent* for it to be acceptable. Thus, its projected incremental cash flows will be discounted at a rate of 20 percent.

The discounted present value of the future cash flows from Satka's required investment—discounted at 20 percent—is diagramed in Figure 8.6. All of the figures in this diagram were computed effortlessly by using Excel's present value function.[8] Across the top of the diagram are each year's forecasted cash flows computed in Figure 8.4. The arrows point to the present value of each cash flow—discounted at 20 percent—on the day that the required investment is made at the beginning of Year-1.

The $220,500 cash flow anticipated by the *end* of Year-1—discounted at 20 percent—has a present value at the beginning of Year-1 of $183,750.

[8]Excel's present value function is extremely user friendly and is by far the most efficient manner in which to determine the present value of an investment's future cash flows. The amounts shown are based on a discount rate of 20 percent *compounded annually*. Alternatives to *Excel* include financial calculators, present value tables, and the use of present value formulas.

This simply means that $183,750 invested at 20 percent at the beginning of Year-1 will grow to $220,500 by the end of Year-1. Likewise, the $285,320 cash flow expected by the end of Year-2—discounted at 20 percent—has a present value of $198,139 at the beginning of Year-1. In other words, $198,139 invested at 20 percent at the beginning of Year-1 will grow to $285,320 by the end of Year-2. The $245,000 cash flow anticipated in Year-3 has a present value of $141,782, meaning that $141,782 invested at 20 percent at the beginning of Year-1 will grow to $245,000 by the end of Year-3. Finally, the $260,535 cash flow anticipated in Year-4 has a present value of $125,644, meaning that $125,644 invested at 20 percent at the beginning of Year-1 will grow to $260,535 by the end of Year-4.

Although the investment's total projected cash flow over the 4-year period is $1,011,354, the total *present value* of those cash flows, as shown in Figure 8.6, is only $649,315. Said differently, if Satka desires a return of 20 percent, it should be willing to invest *up to* $649,315 for the required equipment. Fortunately, the *cost* of the investment is only $625,000—not $649,315—so the equipment's *NPV* is $24,315. A *positive* NPV means that an investment's *actual return*—referred to as its *IRR*—is expected to be *greater* than the required return used as a discount rate. Figure 8.6 conveys an IRR on this investment of *22 percent*, which is 2 percent higher than the 20 percent required return that Satka used as a discount rate.[9]

NPV and IRR Relationships

An investment's NPV and IRR are related to each other as follows:

- If an investment's NPV is *positive*, its IRR is *greater than* the discount rate.
- If an investment's NPV is *zero*, its IRR *equals* the discount rate.
- If an investment's NPV is *negative*, its IRR is *less than* the discount rate.

These relationships are illustrated in Figure 8.7. The left column of the illustration lists the forecasted cash flows computed in Figure 8.4.

[9]The 22 percent IRR figure was computed effortlessly using *Excel*'s internal rate of return function.

Annual Projected Cash Flow		Discounted @ 20%	Discounted @ 22%	Discounted @ 25%
Year-1 = $220,500	→	$ 183,750	$ 180,743	$ 176,400
Year-2 = $285,320	→	198,139	$ 191,706	$ 182,605
Year-3 = $245,000	→	141,782	$ 134,934	$ 125,440
Year-4 = $260,535	→	125,644	117,618	106,715
Total Present Values		$ 649,315	$ 625,000	$ 591,160
Cost of Investment		(625,000)	(625,000)	(625,000)
Net Present Values (NPV)		**$ 24,315**	**$ (0)**	**$ (33,840)**
Internal Rates of Return (IRR)		**22%**	**22%**	**22%**

***Figure 8.7** NPV & IRR: comparisons across multiple discount rates*

The arrows point to the discounted present values of each cash flow at three different discount rates—*20 percent*, *22 percent*, and *25 percent*. It is important to realize that changing the discount rate has *no effect* on the cash flow amounts anticipated in each year. Moreover, changing the discount rate has *no effect* on Satka' $625,000 investment cost. Thus, regardless of what discount rate is used, the investment's IRR remains 22 percent, as shown.

When discounted at 20 percent, its positive NPV of $24,315 shown in Figure 8.7 is exactly the same as it was in Figure 8.6. The NPV is positive because the investment's IRR of 22 percent exceeds Satka's 20 percent discount rate. Had Satka required a 22 percent return, the cash flows would have been discounted 22 percent, and their total present value would have *exactly equaled* the investment's $625,000 cost, resulting in an NPV of *zero*—which is marginally acceptable. Finally, had Satka required a 25 percent return, the cash flows would have been discounted at *25 percent*, and their total present value would have been only $591,160. Using a discount rate that *exceeds* the investment's IRR by 2 percent would have resulted in a *negative* NPV of $33,840—which is *unacceptable*.

Nonfinancial Issues

In addition to financial concerns, all capital investments also involve nonfinancial issues that must be taken into consideration. Unlike financial concerns, nonfinancial issues are often subjective, making their effects difficult to measure.

Nonfinancial issues often involve environmental, ethical, legal, socio-economic, race, gender, and morale-related considerations. Satka's decision of whether to invest in machinery so that an idle production facility can be used to produce components for military weapons encompasses several unique nonfinancial issues. These issues include potential security threats, political repercussions, liability exposure, reputation perceptions, and patriotic responsibility.

Summary

This chapter examined the basic concepts and practices involving the capital budgeting process. Managers use capital budgets to evaluate and prioritize large, and sometimes very risky, capital investment opportunities.

The primary focus of the capital budgeting process is on the incremental effects of an investment opportunity—the most critical elements of which involve forecasting its incremental cash flows and establishing the minimum return required to compensate a company for the investment's inherent risks.

Time-value-of-money concepts, and tradeoffs between risk and return, play a key role in determining a capital investment's present value. An investment's present value is a measure of its financial desirability. Present values are a function of the amount of cash a capital investment is expected to generate, how quickly the cash will be generated, and likelihood that the investment's cash benefits will actually materialize. Generally speaking, investments with a potential to generate large amounts of cash flow, in short amounts of time, with relatively low risk, have higher present values than riskier investments that take more time to generate less cash flow.

All three capital budgeting measures illustrated in this chapter—the payback period, NPV, and IRR—are widely used to evaluate capital investment decisions. Of these measures, NPV and IRR take into consideration the time-value of money. When an investment's IRR exceeds the discount rate used to compensate a company for risk, the investment's NPV will be positive, and therefore financially desirable. Conversely, if an investment's IRR is less than the discount rate used to compensate a company for risk, the investment's NPV will be negative, and therefore financially undesirable.

Finally, it is important to bear in mind that nonfinancial issues sometimes make financially desirable investments unacceptable. Likewise, they also can make financially undesirable investments a necessity.

About the Author

Mark Bettner is the Christian R. Lindback professor of accounting and financial management in the College of Management at Bucknell University. He received his PhD in business administration from Texas Tech University in 1988, his MS in accountancy from Virginia Tech in 1982, and his BS in business administration from Oregon State University in 1980. Mark is an author of several widely used accounting textbooks and has published numerous scholarly and practitioner articles. He is a reviewer for a wide range of academic journals, including *The International Journal of Accounting, Business, & Society*; *The International Journal of Business & Accounting*; *Advances in Public Interest Accounting*; *Essays in Economics & Business History*; *Critical Perspectives on Accounting*; and *The International Journal on Critical Accounting.* He also offers a professional development course each summer at Penn State University for the Pennsylvania Bankers Association.

Mark and his wife, Francoise, have resided in Lewisburg for 30 years. They are the proud parents of four grown children and three partially grown grandchildren.

Index

OTHER TITLES IN OUR FINANCIAL ACCOUNTING AND AUDITING COLLECTION

Mark Bettner, Bucknell University and
Michael Coyne, Fairfield University, *Editors*

- *Accounting for Fun and Profit: A Guide to Understanding Advanced Topics in Accounting* by Lawrence A. Weiss
- *Accounting History and the Rise of Civilization, Volume I* by Gary Giroux
- *Accounting History and the Rise of Civilization, Volume II* by Gary Giroux
- *A Refresher in Financial Accounting* by Faisal Sheikh
- *Accounting Fraud, Second Edition: Maneuvering and Manipulation, Past and Present* by Gary Giroux
- *Corporate Governance in the Aftermath of the Global Financial Crisis, Volume I: Relevance and Reforms* by Zabihollah Rezaee
- *Corporate Governance in the Aftermath of the Global Financial Crisis, Volume II: Functions and Sustainability* by Zabihollah Rezaee
- *Corporate Governance in the Aftermath of the Global Financial Crisis, Volume III: Gatekeeper Functions* by Zabihollah Rezaee
- *Corporate Governance in the Aftermath of the Global Financial Crisis, Volume IV: Emerging Issues in Corporate Governance* by Zabihollah Rezaee